Bletchley and Fenny Tapestry of Thoughts

The Voice of the People

Bletchley People

Copyright © 2024 Jean Flannery
For Bletchley People
ISBN: **9798884559011**

To Miss Bright,
a lovely young lady and very inspirational teacher who has touched our lives and is much loved by our grandson Seb.x

Thank you for the memories that Seb has made in Year One. He will never forget them & who knows one day, he may write his own story.x

I hope this book gives some pleasure and makes you smile.x

DEDICATION

This books is dedicated to all Bletchleyites, born and adoptive, past and present, and to those who inspired us.

Dave McLean
18/7/2024

CONTENTS

Acknowledgements	i
Introduction	1
Getting the Show on the Road	3
The Malcolm Wheeler Story	5
Signature Showcases	16
Conversation Starters	18
People and Places	23
Local Schools	64
Youth Groups	93
Call the Doctor	102
Commemoration	105
Christmas Past	131
Let's Go Shopping	142
Home of the Code Breakers	183
Our Cultural Heritage	196
Love is in the Air	230
The Word on the Street	247
On the Street Where You Lived	261
On the Buses	282
Horses Remembered	291
The Passing of Steam - The End of an Era	297
Afterword	302

BLETCHLEY AND FENNY TAPESTRY OF THOUGHTS

ACKNOWLEDGMENTS

With grateful thanks to all whose names appear in this book and to every member of the "Bletchley & Fenny Where are They Now?" Facebook group. Without your memories, your input and interest, this book would never have come into being.

INTRODUCTION

All the stories, anecdotes and photos in this book are contributions from members of the Facebook group "Bletchley & Fenny Where Are They Now?"

In January 2017 Malcolm Wheeler and Joy (Payne) Doyle were inspired to create this group for those of us who attended school in the Bletchley area at any time. From small beginnings, the group now comprises some 1.5 thousand members and is growing every week. We all owe Malcolm and Joy a real debt of gratitude.

Diane McLean was invited by Malcolm Wheeler to join the admin team in April 2022. Enthusiastic and ever encouraging, Diane has enlivened us all with her ideas for "showcases" as will be seen.

I met Diane via the group and we very soon developed a real friendship, being likeminded and having much in common. That friendship has grown to the point where we quite frequently find ourselves thinking along the same lines.

The idea for this book came almost simultaneously to Diane and me. We thought how wonderful it would be to preserve at least some of the memories and thoughts shared with the group by its members.

Diane devised chapters and chose most of the stories and pictures to include, a far from easy job given all the quality material to consider. But we couldn't include it all and so difficult choices did have to be made. Malcolm, Diane and I agreed on the "final cut" - for this book at least.

I chose some stories and photos, collated, compiled, edited and generally put the book together ready for publication. Again, the three of us agreed on the result. It has been a real collaborative effort.

Our hope is that you enjoy this glimpse into the lives of those of us who have at some time known the Bletchley and Fenny area as home.

Where are we now? Wherever in the world we live, a part of our heart remains in Bletchley.

The only profit from sales of this book will be Amazon's, required as a condition of publication. There will be no royalties.

Jean Blane Flannery

GETTING THE SHOW ON THE ROAD

<u>18 January 2017 - The Start of Something Special</u>

The "Bletchley and Fenny Where Are They Now?" group was formed with a small team of founder members 18 January 2017. The Signature photo was posted and "A Star was Born," a star that has been guided by one leading light: Malcolm Wheeler.

Malcolm's calm, consistent approach has steered the group to where it is today. His equitable, approachable manner and sense of humour make him a real pleasure to work with, and he has indeed built a group that grows from strength to strength.

Throughout the life of the group there have inevitably been many occasions when members have organised their own "friends reunited" gatherings, which have always been well supported with new friendships resulting from them.

In October 2023 the group held its first official "Memory Lane Get-together" and what a perfect day it was, after much excitement and anticipation. It was humbling how far many people had travelled to support the event, which was the "Talk of the Town." It was an event where local history was written.

"A Listers" are our celebrated members who appear on the Signature photo. To get four of our "A Listers" together in one place after almost seventy years was indeed very special.

Back: Michael Willet and Glyn Lewis
Front: Sue and Ken Dobson

It tugged at the heartstrings to see how many of our members arrived at the event with envelopes, ring binders and treasured family photograph albums, all stuffed with memorabilia to share.

Numbers on the roll of honour exceeded 100: members who wore their badges with pride, wanting to share "thoughts of yesteryear" quite literally.

To Infinity and Beyond...

Diane McLean

THE MALCOLM WHEELER STORY

I was born 14 November 1949 to Marjorie Diamond and Donald Edwin Wheeler at 14 Bedford Street Bletchley, the home of my grandparents Mary and Walter Upton. Nurse Cameron was the midwife, assisted by my grandmother who we all called Mama.

I recently realised that father was not present at my birth or my first Christmas, as he was on National Service in Meniden Germany.

14 Bedford Street was a large 3 bedroom house, the bathroom lit by gas light. The downstairs had a front room, sitting room, and a day room with a wonderful black iron coal heated range, which really warmed the room and also heated the water. In the kitchen was a large brick coal heated boiler for washing clothes. The sink tap was supplied with rainwater from a tank above.

Outside the kitchen was a large, covered area called the harbour. There stood a large bucket, bowls and a galvanised tank that was used to wash clothes by plunging and turning a "ponch" into it. A washboard and large wooden roller mangle were used to wring out the clothes afterwards.

My grandmother Mary Upton hanging out the washing

There was a small outside toilet next to a coal barn and chickens were kept in a coop in the small garden.

I have many happy memories of playing in and around Bedford Street. Mrs Bates and her son Alan lived at number 16. I often used to take their large Alsatian dog Beauty for a walk. But then one day Beauty bit the insurance man in his *"privates."* After that I was not allowed to walk the dog.

Alan was an ice-cream van salesman and I would often accompany him on his rounds. He later took the "Mr Softy" franchise for the area until he emigrated with his wife to Australia.

Across the road from 14 Bedford Street was a large vegetable plot where Sheila Perry lived. There were a couple of old railway carriages in the garden, where we would often play.

When Dad finished his National Service we moved into our first family house at 39 North Street, Bletchley. I have memories of playing there with my first friends, Alan Rouse and Dennis Westly.

At the bottom of North Street was the original United Counties bus depot and the Civil Defense training building, which was often set on fire to help train the CD. We boys often climbed over the gate.

If a bus had been left unlocked we played at being bus conductors or drivers. Occasionally we found a reel of bus tickets and would then argue over who was going to be the conductor.

We often had tramps or travellers knocking on the door for some sugar or something to eat. The knife sharpener, with his bicycle back wheel specially adapted so he could turn a grindstone to sharpen knives and scissors etc, came round every year.

I remember Dad decorating the house with bunting for Queen Elizabeth's coronation in June 1953. There was a party in the offices of Asphaltic Company, at the bottom of what became Tavistock Street. We were all given a five-shilling piece as a memento.

Our first television arrived in time for the big day, and everyone sat down to watch it on what must have been an 8-inch screen.

I have many happy memories of playing in the garden of my grandparents at 14 Bedford Street with my cousins Colin and Michael Able. But the greatest times were when my other cousins came down from Nottingham to stay for a week or weekend.

I am playing in the garden with my cousins in the following photo.

In February 1955 my late sister Jennifer was born, and as 39 North Steet only had two bedrooms we swopped with the Rouses who lived at 26, just across the road. So no removal men were needed.

On cold winter days the windows froze and without central heating the touch of cold lino when you got out of bed was a shock to the system. I stood in front of the gas oven to keep warm while getting dressed for school.

Dad grew vegetables in the back garden and had an allotment on what a is now Quick Fit Tyres. Number 26 backed onto a gravel pit where the local anglers spent hours waiting for a bite. It was a great area to play games like Cowboys and Indians.

Sometimes we found an old discarded pram or push chair. This gave my cousins Keith and Trevor Wheeler the opportunity to make a soap box: great fun.

Grandad and Grandma Wheeler lived in Brooklands Road. Grandad had a big garden, with pigs and chickens at the back. I was once asked to catch a chicken for dinner and chased one round the chicken coop for ages until I caught it for grandad to pull its neck.

For bonfire night, dad allowed me to build an enormous bonfire from old trees we chopped down at the side of the cycle track that ran from Tavistock Street to Denbigh Way. We used a truck to collect all the old cardboard and paper waste from the shops on Bletchley Road. This ensured the bonfire would light easily.

I don't remember too much of my infant school or teachers, though I do remember some friends: Stuart Frazer, Barry Bates, Neil Dick, Neil Felce, Roger Sinfield, John Harris, Christine Harvey, Elizabeth Dymka, Pauline Simpson, Valerie Howlett, Valarie Pacey, Sheila Perry, John Denton, Barry Birtles, John Mc Gee and David Stevens.

School Photo

Barry Bates and I were quite good friends in the junior school and used to play at each other's houses during school holidays. I recall one day when we were only 8 or 9 we cycled to Newport Pagnell to see the Austin Martin Factory.

Barry had a car that he used to drive around the Beacon Brush factory site. During one school holiday Barry and I got a job packing brushes, which is when I received my first week's wages and a large box of various brushes. (I still have some in use today.) Barry passed the 11 plus and went off to grammar school. We then drifted apart and lost contact, as happens with so many school friends.

Once a year the Royal Green Jackets set up a recruitment tent opposite the Bletchley Arms pub. Us boys took it in turns to queue up to see all the guns and equipment, and to sit behind the Vickers machine gun where we pretended to shoot the "enemy."

I loved to attend the cattle market during school holidays, to help move the livestock from wagons to the selling pens and back again (we never got paid). And I recall Mum taking me to Beatle Drives upstairs in the Co-op hall, happy days.

On market days it was common for us local boys to help off load and load the vans of the stall holders for a few shillings. I managed to get a regular helper's job on the market with a grocer every Thursday and Saturday, usually got paid ten bob for Saturdays and two shillings for Thursdays.

I managed to get a job as a butcher's delivery boy at the Co-op butcher's on a Saturday and Wednesday before school. Quite often I had to go to collect from the Co-op factory in Park Street. I was put off faggots for life having seen how they were made, and the stink was something else. The Co-op butcher's moved across the road to the main Co-op site where a new butchery department was opened, with Reg Cutts as the manager.

There was always a race to collect the meat for delivery to make sure you had the local route. We tried to avoid the route to the Wilberforce Hotel on the corner of Buckingham Road and Cottingham Drive. It was hard work peddling a trade bike full of meat up the hill on Buckingham Road and back.

I attended St Margaret's Church on Bletchley Road, went to Sunday School and became an altar boy. When St Margaret's closed I started to attend St Martin's Church as an altar boy and then became a Sunday School teacher. St Martin's had a youth club that organised trips to the Northampton Granada where we saw Paul & Paula, and I think the Tornados. At Granada Bedford we saw Roy Orbison and Cilla Black amongst others.

Bletchley Road Senior School was where I became friends with Chris Turl, Paul West, Don Worby, and David Waite. Catching the train to Bedford from Fenny Stratford Station, Chris Turl and I "took" a day off school to see the matinée at Granada Bedford, where top of the bill were the Rolling Stones.

I enjoyed woodwork and metalwork but my favourites were art with John Morris, religion and music with Daphne Tofield. In art, Paul West and I produced a work of modern art titled "Sun Burst by Stew Releemem." It hung in the school corridor as artist of the month, earning us both A's in art that year. Choir was great fun. Paul and I couldn't sing but could make a very loud noise. Miss Tofield thought it was wonderful, especially in morning assembly.

I took piano lessons with Mrs Cutts in Cambridge Street and passed a few preliminary examinations. I loved music and still do. We got to attend the NME awards at Wembley and saw all the top groups, including the Beatles.

My first visit to the Wilton Hall with Chris Turl was to see the 60s group The Searchers. After that I think I went every week including to the Wednesday disco, usually with David Waite. At school Dave and I were "Mods."

One Saturday afternoon after we had finished our Co-op butcher's deliveries, we hitch hiked to Dunstable to a shop called Farmers to buy our first pair of desert boots to go with our polished cotton trousers, which we had bought from a stall on Bletchley Market. Having finished our shopping we decided to hitch hike back to Bletchley. After two hours a car finally stopped and it was the same guy who had given us a lift to Dunstable earlier in the day.

School holidays were usually spent either swimming in the then new Queens Pool, or in Brickhill woods with the "Gang." I managed to get a key to the Scout hut so we'd go and play snooker in the 2nd Fenny Stratford Scout hut, behind the Methodist Church on Bletchley Road.

I was in the Kestrel Patrol and my patrol leader was Bob Morgan who lived in Albert Street. Bob and I undertook various Scout hikes together, our longest being a hike around the Lake District with Neil Blake (Sandringham Place) and John (lefty) Wright (Victoria Road). I eventually gained my Scout Cord and went on to become a Cub Scout instructor until 2nd Fenny Stratford Scouts disbanded.

As I approached my 15th birthday I was told that I would not be asked to stay on at school for another year, as some of my friends were doing. With me not really having any idea what I wanted to do, Dad arranged me an interview at Pollard's, the ironmongers on Bletchley Road.

I was offered a job and started work as a junior ironmonger assistant 26 April 1965. Peter Betts, Clifford (Dan) Cook, and Headley Pengelly were amongst my work colleagues, along with John and Bruce Pollard. I used to enjoy window dressing the seasonal displays in the windows. It was a great place to work.

4 April 1966 was the day Queen Elizabeth and the Duke of Edinburgh visited Bletchley. Pete Betts and I were charged with decorating the outside of Pollard's with flags and bunting prior to the visit. Whilst on the balcony my attention was drawn to the girls from Neal's toy shop who were shouting.

Looking over the balcony I saw Angela Richardson with someone I had never seen or noticed before. It was Jane Sutton, who a year later would become my wife. Yes, we were only 17 when we married. In October of that year our son Mark was born at the Westbury Maternity home in Newport Pagnell.

To help the finances I worked part time as a barman at the Bletchley Arms and we spent our first four years of married life living with my parents in North Street. Finally, thanks to Councillor David Lee we became tenants of our first house, a council house at 89 Newton Road, Bletchley.

In August 1970 I joined Bletchley Timber in Simpson Road to manage their new DIY shop, alongside Clive Peerless who ran the timber yard. I cycled there and back from Newton Road, including going home for lunch, until I bought a moped which cut travel time down significantly.

6 March 1972 our daughter Joanne was born in the front bedroom of 89 Newton Road, the day before I took my driving test and a week before I took on a new role for Bletchley Timber - managing Jones and Cocks ironmongers in Aylesbury, which Bletchley Timber was in the process of buying.

In Aylesbury I became member of the "Aylesbury Literary Club, " a "Gentleman's Drinking Club" in Temple Street, of which Lord

Rothschild was president. I was for a short time president of the Aylesbury Chamber of Commerce, until Bletchley Timber sold Jones and Cocks and I was made redundant. Being out of work for a few months and with having a family, times were hard.

I applied for and gained a sales rep job with one of my wholesalers who had supplied garden products to Jones and Cocks, which was a relief. After a year or so I was asked to join L & K Fertilisers in Lincoln as their representative in the Home Counties. On arriving in Lincoln for my induction course, imagine my delight when the Vauxhall Viva they had promised as a company car was in fact a brand new Silver Ford Capri.

I worked my way up in the company, now Sinclair Horticulture, makers of Arthur Bowers Compost etc. I was UK sales manager for several years. But with the restructuring of this business I was again made redundant. However, I was soon re-employed as a sales manager for Professional Compost.

In October 2005 I followed my father and grandfather into freemasonry. Having spent most of my working life travelling across the country, "a man in a suitcase," this gave me the opportunity to reconnect with old school friends.

Becoming Master of Manor of Swanburn Lodge in 2014. I am actively involved in running the Bletchley Masonic Centre and have recently formed a new company to run the bar and dining hall, Bletchley Masonic Events Ltd.

Disaster stuck on Friday 24 October 2014, whilst I was on my way to Crownhill Crematorium to lay flowers on the anniversary of Mum's death. Jane phoned and shouted "FIRE! FIRE!" That was all I could understand so I quickly turned the car around and raced home to find two fire engines there and black billowing smoke.

Our tumble dryer had caught fire, burnt out the kitchen and filled the house with smoke damage. Jane, and Jazz our golden retriever, had just managed to escape and were in the back garden. Thankfully an ambulance driver had seen the fire and racing up the road administered oxygen to Jane. He said that if she had not got out when she did she may have never got out at all, due to smoke getting into her lungs.

After a week, and with thanks to a friend, we managed to find furnished accommodation where we spent the next four months waiting for our insurers to pay up. Whilst on a week's holiday to New York In December our insurance adviser called. He said Santander our insurers were not going to pay out.

It was not until we returned home and read all the documentation that we found the reason for non-payment. The application form asked if we lived within 100yds of water and I had replied "No." However, as the crow flies the Blue Lagoon was just 97 yards away. Taking advice we appealed to the Ombudsman, who agreed with Santander - saying we were out to defraud them!!!

The house was unliveable, so we basically had to start all over again. Thanks to family and friends, after three months we were able to move back in. We had to dip into our pension pot and savings to fund the restoration and replacement of furniture and clothes. In addition I became a "plater," delivering and collecting cars part time until I retired in 2023.

My dad died in August 2023 and I am pleased to say we had resolved our old differences and were once again speaking, after 17 years. He was able to see his grandchildren Mark and Joanne, his great grandchildren Blake, Luke, Alex, and Sophie, and his great grandchildren Grace and Oliver, before his death.

Malcolm Wheeler

SIGNATURE SHOWCASES

It seems like only yesterday that I was introducing myself as "The New Kid on the Block." Bletchley born and bred, I was keen to support stories of people, places and events, both past and present.

On joining the admin team it was my personal goal to showcase local people.

This was fuelled by my own memories of my dearly loved granny, who came to Bletchley at the age of 17. She raised three children and lived to enjoy seeing her eight great grandchildren grow up.

My granny spent 38 years of her life working at the Studio, touching many lives and making memories. She was not alone in that.

Growing up in Newton Road, I was keen to hear stories from others of where we lived, laughed, loved and played, making memories with friends: "The Word on the Street."

As a result our Signature Showcases were born, celebrating our own lives and those of loved ones within the community.

Showcases reflect the sharing of memories that celebrate members' achievements and experiences. They are moments that have touched our lives, helping to keep loved ones from our community remembered.

Our showcases have diversified and grown in popularity over time. Many members have opened their own showcases and many have inspired the creation of others.

They are something that we dip in and out of regularly, with old storylines being revisited and enhanced for our continued enjoyment.

Our Signature Showcases contribute much to the success and popularity of the group.

52 showcases have been opened to date - among our most popular being "Weddings" and "On The Street Where You Lived."

It is from our showcases that we are able to weave our tapestry of thoughts and share the voice of the people.

Diane McLean

CONVERSATION STARTERS

THE PETER JOHN STANLEY STORY

Peter John Stanley is, like myself, Bletchley born and bred. Peter was the third eldest son of parents Ted and Joyce Stanley.

Born in 1956, Peter was one of eight siblings growing up on the Saints estate. Peter was a pupil at Castles, Rivers and Rickley Lane Schools before moving on to Denbigh Secondary School in Cornwall Grove.

He has always been very inquisitive, developing skills that have come into their own and earned him the esteemed title "King of the Conversation Starters."

On leaving school Peter began working for a local firm Alan Bradley, starting out in their stores department and from there moving to an office post.

Peter was a carer for his parents for many years. Sadly his mother died and Peter then cared for his dad, who died six months later.

It wasn't until the age of 40 that Peter had the opportunity to study for a degree in Social Science. Like many members of the group he has been keen to trace his family roots and plot his family tree.

It was his interest in local history that led Peter to join the "Bletchley and Fenny Where Are They Now?" Group. Peter has been a member for six years and during that time has indeed proved his worth. His inquisitive, enquiring mind has enabled him to initiate countless "Conversation Starters."

Many have soared instantly to the top of the "popularity ratings," some have initiated the opening of showcases and two have formed the basis of whole group projects:

What We Miss Most About Bletchley and Fenny Back in the Day

Iconic Buildings Remembered

A block buster that brought a tear to many an eye was this one:

Just thinking of routines we had when I was a child, on a Sunday it was bath night and we would listen to Cliff Michelmore and Jimmy Clitheroe. When it got to seven o'clock and "Sing Something Simple" came on I knew it was time for a bath and bed.

Bathtime went on for a while as Mum had 7 kids under the age of 8 years. Hard work for Mum but as we got older it was less so. I wonder if this happened in other households?

Peter John Stanley

The conversation had started and the ball was rolling...

From the 70 comments I have chosen 7 that to me best reflect "The Voice of the People."

Diane McLean

We lived in a railway house in Loughton, surrounded by fields, so we had a lot of mice. We had an old copper built into the corner of the kitchen. Dad used to fill the bath from this. If he hadn't managed to find coal from the steam trains on the banks, the house was freezing. Or us kids would go "wooding" with an old pram.

We also had oil lamps and candles. When we moved to a temporary cottage we had a cold tap in the yard and at 15 years old I'd wash my hair and clean my teeth under it even in the winter- it would kill young people today.

Josie Mabbutt

Bath-time at my grandparents (who I stayed with often) was a tin bath in front of the fire with a clothes horse around it for privacy. The toilet was outside in the yard. It was a bucket toilet and newspaper squares for wipes. If you wanted to go during the night, you used a pot under the bed.

Maureen Griffiths

Being an only child, for the first seven years I didn't have to share our bath in front of the fire on a Sunday. Dad was a man of routine. At 6am he'd make a pot of tea and hot porridge after lighting the Rayburn.

Most mornings he and I would sit dunking Rich Tea or Digestive biscuits in the warm kitchen, talking of the day's schedule for our small holding or the farm before he went to check, feed and milk the cow and goats. My duty on school days was to collect the milk in the big buckets, bring it home and then get ready for school.

I was out of school uniform the moment I got home, ready to put into action any orders my dad would have left me to do. They were mostly with the animals or on the land. Housework like pot washing was done before playing in the village at the weekend.

My sister Hazel who was born seven years later suffered from asthma and various illnesses from being a baby. So Mum spent a lot of time nursing her or in the kitchen.

The Archers, Mrs Dale's Diary, the News and the Weather Forecast were all "don't disturb" times for our parents. The Clitheroe Kid and Desert Island Discs were for us all.

Early experiences in childhood didn't do me any harm. In fact even today they've stood me in good stead.

Me with my mother

Judith Kutty

We didn't have a bathroom until I was 9. Until then it was a tin bath, and a freezing cold toilet at the bottom of the garden.

Barry Linford

As a child, I was blessed to live next door to my paternal grandparents. We didn't have a bathroom so every Sunday we all

(Mum, Dad and me), went next door for a bath! Kids today have no idea! I remember all the radio programmes mentioned.

Happy Carefree Days

Ann Elliott Stephens

Exactly the same for us and a wash-house in the back yard, also the "lavender lorry" collecting from the toilet tank every week.

Alan Andrews

We had the boiler on once a week to heat the water, until the house was renovated by the council long after I moved out. Before school I had a top and tail in the kitchen, after boiling the kettle.

If I wanted a bath during the week, when I was a teenager, I had to carry buckets of hot water up the stairs. We never had an inside toilet all the time I lived there. And I was born there.

Mary Church Hazell

Reading all of the stories was very humbling: were they really "the good old days?" It is lovely to have the happy memories. And what is so special about the group is that we can all feel safe in sharing our stories.

This book is all about "The Voice Of The People." We hope you enjoy your journey.

"Buckle up tight - parts of the ride might be a little bit bumpy..."

Diane McLean

PEOPLE AND PLACES

KEN AND SUE DOBSON

Two members with celebrity status are Ken Dobson and Sue Allan. They are quite rightly referred to as our very own "A" Listers. Two faces from our cover photo, two pupils who were in the same class, two friends who on leaving Bletchley Road School at the age of 15 began a romance that truly blossomed.

Ken and Sue were married at St Marys Church Bletchley at 4pm on Saturday 28 June 1969. They had six bridesmaids attending.

It was a beautiful hot day and the reception for 100 guests was held at the Coronation Hall. Mrs Strickland catered the reception.

The cake came from the Co-op. Ken had not perfected his skills at this stage.

It was later that he began making celebration cakes for his family. For his own daughter Ken created a seven tier masterpiece.

A very talented family, the entertainment at the reception was music performed by Sue's Uncle Harold Brewer and her cousin Barry. Harold played the piano while Barry at the very young age of 7 years played the drums.

Ken and Sue shared this lovely story with us just one week before the "Memory Lane Get Together," when history was made and all four of our "A" listers were reunited after so many years.

Diane McLean

Sue and I renewing our wedding vows on our 50th wedding anniversary, five years ago.

Ken Dobson

MICHAEL WILLETT

I was born at the Barratt Maternity Unit in Northampton to Doris Gee and Mark Willett 25 August 1949. At the age of 5 I started school at Manor Road Infants, the headmistress Mrs Bramham. Mum recalls that when she picked me up on my first day, she asked me if I liked it. I said it was "OK but I don't think I will do it again."

At 7 years old I went to Saffron Street Junior School, where my teacher was the lovely Miss Joan West who had worked at Bletchley Park during the war. They were happy days.

Michael's junior class with his favourite teacher Miss West

I went up to the big school when I was 11 years old, where I now wore long trousers. We had separate girls and boys playgrounds for the first two years I was there, then they were combined. Among my teachers were Mr Rose, Mr Puryer, Mr Cross, Mr Ripley, Mr Brown and three called Jones - Jotter, Horace and Buck.

When in July 1964 at aged 14 we broke up for the summer holidays, I decided school wasn't for me. With advice from my father I successfully applied for an apprenticeship at Wolverton Works. The only problem was that the intake for new apprentices was the beginning of August.

I wasn't old enough to work full time until I was 15 at the end of August, so I had to wait. Then at the age of 15 I stepped into the real world. What a shock I had. My leisure time during the next five years still involved football, table tennis, cricket - but now also included, naturally, girls. When at the age of 21 my apprenticeship finished, I was offered a job in the millwrights' department.

When I was 20 I became engaged and saved hard, eventually purchasing a bungalow in Newport Pagnell for the exorbitant price of £4,000. After marriage I still spent time with my two best mates, Glyn Lewis and John Thurston. I had two sons, Sam and Stephen, who both enjoyed the same sports as I did and both played to a reasonable standard.

I left the railways around 1980 and ran my own business for a number of years, before returning to Wolverton Works in 1995.

Following the breakup of my marriage and taking early retirement, I was lucky enough to meet up with the lady in my life: the lovely Michelle. We have spent the last ten years living the quiet life in lovely rural Lincolnshire.

Michael Willett   A proud group A Lister

THE GLYN LEWIS STORY

Glyn Lewis, one of the group's A Listers, was born in March 1949 at the Red House in Fenny Stratford. Glyn had a difficult start in life. This from a local minister:

"On May 1st I was summoned to baptize privately a little baby, Glyn Lewis. He seemed very near the end. However, he was taken to Great Ormonde (sic) Street Hospital and his parents now have reassuring news. GOD's Hand was certainly stretched forth to heal him.   C.A.W"

Known then as a blue baby, Glyn was indeed rushed to Great Ormond Street Hospital, where he was luckily given excellent care and treatment and has lived to tell the tale. That is exactly what he has done. I am proud and privileged to bring you his story.

Glyn was the youngest son of Joan and Bernard (Taffy) Lewis, who met and fell in love whilst working together at the local brush factory.

Sadly, Glyn never knew his grandmother who died at a very young age. He does however have fond memories of his grandad, Albert Edward Millard. Glyn was very close to his grandad, whom he affectionately refers to as Gramps.

Albert was a man ahead of his time, owning a car before many others in the town. He was quite a character in many respects with a wide circle of interesting friends, one being the hangman at Bedford prison.

Albert worked for Garner and Son on Denmark Street, a firm originally from London. He continued working long after retirement age and held many part time jobs. One of those was helping to build coffins and laying people out ready for viewing or burial. He ended his days peacefully and happily in a cottage in Victoria Road.

Albert proudly wearing his RFC uniform.

The family lived with Albert at 73 Simpson Road and it was there that Glyn grew up and his early childhood memories were made.

A memory that has stuck in Glyn's mind and never fails to raise a smile is the day the local pub, the White Hart, was giving away ice creams. For whatever reason, the landlord needed to be shot of them.

Glyn and his mates willingly took them off his hands, much to the dismay of Mrs Lewis who had no refrigerator merely a cold marble slab, like most homes. So melted ice cream was the dish of the day.

When Glyn was 11 years old his parents were offered a house in Whiteley Crescent. This was a move from one end of the town to the other. His dad was moving back to his home turf, closer to the Lewis Dynasty.

Albert in the Whiteley Crescent garden

Bernard had grown up in Newton Road with his sisters Thelma, Olwen, Eileen and Beryl. Beryl Lewis lived all her life in Newton Road where she raised her family. Eileen married Jack Moseley and they ran the White Hart in Simpson Road, then moving to The Bridge in Fenny. They were later offered the tenancy of a brand new pub, taking the name with them - the White Hart now located on Whaddon Way.

Glyn spent a year at Holne Chase junior school and went from there to Wilton Secondary School. Glyn's parents were not happy with his progress and after a while he made a fresh start at Bletchley Road School, hence earning a place on the group's cover photo.

The rest is history as they say and Glyn remained happily there until he left at the ripe old age of 15 years, beginning his career path with Barclays Bank Stationery.

Diane McLean

PC KENNY

My dad is Patrick (Pat) Kenny, best known to some of you as PC 528 Kenny, long-standing area beat officer for Fenny Stratford and Bletchley. Dad started his police career in the British Transport Police. He was stationed at Paddington and that's where he met my mum, who was also a police officer at the time.

Mum and Dad married in 1955 and I was born 9 months later. Dad transferred to Bucks Constabulary and 3 weeks after my birth we moved into one of the 4 police houses in Whaddon Way.

The police station at that time was in Fenny Stratford, just before the railway crossing. Dad was more than happy to be an area beat officer. If he wasn't pedalling his bike in the area then he could be found there pounding the beat. He knew his area inside out, all of the businesses and people. He loved his job even though it rarely ended when his shift did. At any hour people would knock on our door wanting his help or to report something.

Dad got to be on duty when all the up and coming groups of the 60s came to town. In fact, he was invited into the Rolling Stones' dressing room for a drink after asking them to move some of their equipment as it was causing an obstruction. He insists he declined the offer.

Dad was present at the scene of the Great Train Robbery and it was his job to guard the farmhouse the robbers had holed up in. It was exciting to see Dad shown in a piece of film on the news that evening. He was also instrumental in providing the local intelligence that identified the offender of the "Clockwork Orange Murder" in the early 1970s, enabling him to be brought to justice.

At times Dad took over other officers' roles if needed. One was the Coroner's Officer, a role that needs someone with a special kind of temperament. Dad found the role suited him very well. When the post became vacant Dad was offered the job. He accepted and that's where he stayed until the end of his career.

He shunned chances of promotion over the years, just wanting to be an officer for the people. He treated everyone with respect.

Dad experienced many changes over the years, not least the growth of Milton Keynes. Bucks Constabulary eventually became Thames Valley Police, Fenny Stratford police station closed, and over time the only police station became that in the city centre.

Dad was a devoted husband and father, loving and kind; a quiet man but with a wicked sense of humour. Above all else, he was a real family man.

In my early years Dad regularly took part in tug o' war matches as an anchor man for the police team. We'd sometimes go to cheer him on. I remember going to watch him once when I was very little, crying and calling out, "Don't hurt my daddy" as the rest of team all fell on him.

Dad's other interests included organising the Police Ball every November (although planning took all year). This was a major event, always featuring a big band and support group. Bob Miller and his Millermen were a big favourite. Bob and my parents became firm friends over the years. For several years Dad also organised the Catholic Spring Ball at the Labour Hall.

On retirement, Dad got a part time job with Milton Keynes Council. But very sadly the happy retirement he hoped to have with my beloved mum was dashed when Mum became ill and passed on 18 months later.

Dad lived in Bletchley for the rest of his days - loved, cared for and entertained by his four daughters, sons-in-law, grandchildren and great grandchildren, to whom he will always be a hero.

Louise Carey

PC Kenny was a wonderful man. As children we had the greatest respect for him. He was always ready to speak to us.

As an adult and understanding how good he was, that respect and admiration only grew. When he became Coroner the post couldn't have gone to a more trusted, conscientious and loved person.

He will never be forgotten by us locals.

Teresa Skinner

I remember Pat Kenny riding around on his bicycle - a visible but kindly presence. Len and one of his colleagues used to come regularly and talk to my class at St Thomas Aquinas School about their work as police officers. The children loved their visits.

Pauline Thompson

Len Woodley, retired policeman and local author

Len was a friend, colleague and at one time neighbour of Pat Kenny. His very poignant words tugged at my heartstrings and made me want to share them with you.

" Pat was a conscientious policeman who went about his work in a quiet manner and was utterly reliable. He was respected by all who knew him, from constables to chief superintendents, from members of the public to coroners, and his work on the Fenny murder case shows the value of a "good copper" knowing the beat for which he is responsible; getting to know the people, gaining their trust and going about his business without fuss."

What a lovely tribute to a much loved local hero.

Diane McLean

ALAN BUGLASS AND THE TIN SHOPS

Alan Buglass 1936 - 2011

Alan Buglass moved to Bletchley as a young married man seeking employment. He raised his family in the town and his daughter Lisa Wilkinson tells how her dad was a massive Tottenham Hotspur fan and how much she loved going to see the matches with him.

Lisa describes her dad as a loving husband, father and grandfather, who was much loved and is sadly missed by his family and friends. We see Alan looking very happy here in the role of Best Man to a work colleague.

Alan worked at Westland Helicopters, as a polisher at Kemble's, and for the last few years of his working life was employed at Caton House. He earned his place in local history as "the man on the bike."

Alan on his bike driving past the tin huts in Bletchley Road: the iconic shot of the flyover.

Diane McLean

One of the tin shops - not quite the kind of bike Alan is riding!

TERRY FOSTER

Fenny Lock cottage early 1900s, the home of lock keeper Grandpa Foster and Grandma who are pictured, and the childhood home of my dad Bill Foster

Terry Foster

Moving forward several decades, Terry was growing up in Oxford Street before becoming well known to many as a local "bobby on the beat" and later a patrol officer.

A few of the local lads are admiring Terry's patrol car, mid 1970s.

Friendly and approachable, helping people in whatever way he could, Terry is very fondly remembered. But he wouldn't turn a blind eye to criminality, so if you were up to no good you might get "your collar felt" by him.

A modest man, Terry wouldn't ever blow his own trumpet. But he also served the Bletchley community through his work with Rotary and the Masons.

Beyond that, Terry served on the School Board of Knowles junior and middle schools for a number of years. He was Chairman for around eight of those years, a role he filled well.

Here is Terry on the left opening a school fête.

Knowles Middle School came into being 1 September 1973, the name take from "Knowles Field" on a local tythe map.

Jean Blane Flannery

DAVID BRUCE RESCUE

This is story of bravery that will tug at your heartstrings.

David Bruce made local headlines in 1960 for rescuing a young boy from drowning. David received an award in recognition for this very heroic and brave deed.

Diane McLean

"A six-years-old boy who fell into the rain-swollen brook in Water Eaton on Sunday, was saved from drowning by a 12-years-old youngster who waded into the fast-flowing flood, although he cannot swim.

None the worse apart from a heavy cold for his narrow escape Paul Smale, who attends Manor Road Infants' School and who lives with his parents in Willow Way, Bletchley, told a Gazette reporter how he was saved by David Bruce, of Westfield Road, Bletchley."

Rescue excitement behind them, David (left) and Paul enjoy a quieter game: Bletchley District Gazette 10 December 1960

JOANNE BATHAM A GREAT FUND RAISING EFFORT

"Little Joanne Batham popped a half-penny Into a bag every time the sun shone during the past year. She asked her family and friends to do the same and the result was 2,400 coins - which meant £12 in her bag for charity.

The sunshine bags were the Idea of pensioners Albert and Majorie Harrington, senior members of Toc H in Bletchley and neighbours of Joanne.

Joanne aged nine, of Tavistock Street, Bletchley, said: 'The sun didn't shine much during the year so I asked other people to put money in the sunshine bags when It did.' It was the first time she had joined in the sunshine scheme and she plans to do it again.

Joanne, who attends Knowles Middle School, Bletchley, collected the most money among local Toc H members and presented £180 for the planned Willen Hospice in Milton Keynes."

Milton Keynes Gazette 18 July 1979

My daughter Jojo collecting money in her sunshine bag for TOC H

Sheila Batham

JOYCE CLEMENTS

I wonder how many of us remember the days when the town could proudly present us with Miss Bletchley.

Seen here is the beautiful Joyce Clements when she was awarded the title in 1948.

Joyce was born 3 August 1924, the daughter of George and Jessie Clements. She had a brother called Rex, who played in a local band.

Many may remember Rex, who sadly passed away at the young age of 44. The family lived in Napier Street and Joyce later moved to

Albert Street. I know she is fondly remembered by her old school friends. Sadly Joyce herself died in 2010.

Joyce had 4 children - 3 sons and a daughter. The lovely Annette at age 18 years, in a photo taken by the legendary Raymond Lubbock, is seen here alongside her mother.

Annette, with Joyce wearing her Miss Bletchley sash

Diane McLean

JACK HOBBS

My late father-in-law Jack Hobbs

After leaving school Jack was an apprentice butcher at the Co-op, as you see him on the left in this picture.

His national service interrupted this and once he had served his time in the RAF he started work at Bletchley Printers.

It was there he met his wife Mary. Easter Sunday this year, 2023, would have been their 68th wedding anniversary.

Dave Harris

I think the other man may be Archie White, who was working at the Co-op butcher's shop next to the Park Hotel where my Uncle Reg Cutts was manager.

Jean Blane Flannery

SIDNEY AND ALICE SANDS

My maternal grandparents log hauling for Rowlands Timber in Fenny, the year unknown.

My grandfather Sidney was owner operator of this 6 tonne Foster compound engine. Although having one of the cottages at the bottom of Brooklands Road they travelled around in the living van with Mum, Aunt Audrey and Uncles Ted and Ralph.

The face you can just see in the van's right hand window is my sister Judy, from when we visited them as kids.

Nobby Clark

THE MIGHTY QUINN

Local football was a joy to watch in those days. I remember the local derbys between Bletchley United and Wolverton town.

There were big crowds as well, no trouble at all except Mrs Quinn and her rattle, lovely lady.

Mrs Quinn - "The Mighty Quinn" - in action.

Michael Willett

HERBERT SELLEN

As with many others, it was due to the effects of WWII that Herbert made his home in Bletchley. However, unlike most Herbert wasn't a Londoner and didn't move to the town during or after the war.

Herbert was a Canadian, visiting his daughter Phyllis Fryer at her home 59 Eaton Avenue when war broke out and he was unable to return to Canada.

59 Eaton Avenue

Herbert stayed in Bletchley, living with his daughter. He soon became a familiar sight to the residents, riding around the town on his racing bike. During the war he ran art classes in Bletchley and provided artwork for local newspapers.

During the war Herbert ran several art classes in Bletchley and also provided artwork for the local newspapers. However, he was also a renowned artist and illustrator with a far reaching reputation. His illustrations for the children's book, "The Story Of Little Greedy," are among his best known work.

Herbert continued to live with his daughter at her home in Eaton Avenue until his death in 1962, aged 86.

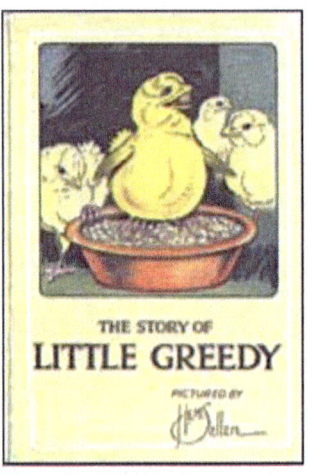

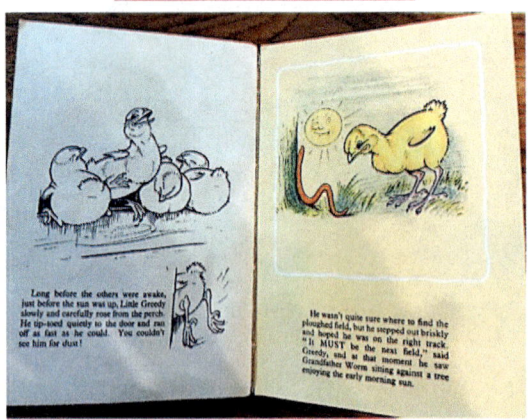

Herbert's granddaughter is Kathleen Fryer, who grew up to become an art teacher at Bletchley Grammar School and whose own artistic talent was perhaps inspired and encouraged by her grandfather. Was it also something handed down?

Jean Blane Flannery

MR TATTAM AND CENTRAL GARDENS

An old photograph of Central Gardens.

Looking towards Western Road, tennis courts to left with Cambridge Street out of sight beyond.

North Bucks Times article of 1962

"25 YEARS OF LOOKING AFTER TOWN GARDENS

Groundsman at Central Gardens, Bletchley, for the past 25 years, Mr. George William Tattam retired on Saturday.

Mr. Tattam was the first full-time groundsman and gardener at Central Gardens, and he will retire with the best wishes of all those who have admired the appearance of the gardens from year to year and also of those who have regularly used its ever-increasing sports facilities.

Mr. Tattam, who lives in Western Road, just behind the gardens, worked on the Leon estate for 17 years and still thinks of the good fortune he had in finding a job with the Council just when that estate was being broken up. Over the years he has made many friends, and seen a number of changes. "When I came in 1937, there were just four tennis courts and the path through the gardens. Most of the place was just a wilderness," he says.

There are now eight tennis courts, a bowling green, and a miniature golf course, complete with bunkers.

After the war, a croquet course was also built for the old people, but when the car park was enlarged and the new entrance gates erected this had to go.

Mr. Tattam recalls that fantastic crowds were sometimes seen waiting for a turn on the miniature golf course during the war years. "In one year we had 11,000 people go on the course. It was quite regular to have hundreds here on a Sunday," he says.

As he was being interviewed while still at work last week, Mr. Tattam said "I'll soon tell you how many tickets I've issued for the golf course in my 25 years." He just delved into a box to fetch out a book of tickets - " 49,385," he announced.

"There has not been all that much change in the type of people coming here, only in their dress," he says. "Of course, we get a few of the 'teddy-boy' types kicking up now and again, but nothing serious at all.

I've made many friends, and most of them remember me after they have been away for a long time. Of course, you get your ups and downs wherever you go, but it's the ups I'll remember."

Mr George Tattam (seated) who recently retired from the Council staff, received a kitchen table and chairs from the Council staff and colleagues on Friday. With him are Messrs A Payne, F Neville, P O'Brien, L Windhamouth and F Toms."

George Tattam was my grandad. He lived around the corner at 143 Western Road and this shows him in his garden there.

George helped transform a wilderness into a much loved place. I'm in another group where "Teddy Boys" of yesteryear frequently post photos of themselves in their younger days. They're all respectable men in their 70s and 80s now.

Mark Tattam

I knew your grandad, a lovely man. I was born in Western Road and walked through Central Gardens every day to visit my grandparents in Eaton Avenue. Mr Tattam would let me walk, run and play on his lovely lawns. I have since learnt that was a privilege.

He was kind to me - and always made time for my imaginary friends (Marlene and Michaleno). When I moved to Newton Road I left them in his care. My family have never forgotten his kindness

I wish some of those "Teddy Boys" would come clean - how lovely if they were members of our group.

Diane McClean

He lived opposite me in Western Road, and was always chasing us away when we played football on his lovely grass!

Glyn Ottery

I've heard he was strict. He must have really liked Diane to let her walk on the grass.

He kept his house very neat and tidy as well. It's such a shame someone thought it would be "progress" to get rid of the gardens. People need green space.

Mark Tattam

My Aunt and Uncle Cutts' garden in Cambridge Street backed onto the Central Gardens. We'd sometimes watch the tennis and it wasn't that unusual for a ball to come over the high netting into the garden, impossible to throw back I'm afraid. I have to say though that we children didn't mind!

When we lived in Western Road I walked through the lovely Central Gardens so many times between home and Bletchley Road - lovely memories.

Jean Blane Flannery

Great photos: I grew up in Western Rd. I loved the Central Gardens, clean and well-kept by very dedicated Mr Tattam. He was strict with us kids and a proud man. Happy days!

Margaret McCracken Hogg

The putting greens were brilliant too.

I used to go and watch my Uncle Joe play with Woburn Sands band on a Sunday, maybe get a glass of pop in the Bletchley Arms.

John Sheaf

You can see Mr Tattam on the right in this photo

GREENWAYS

When I was a teenager in the 1960s, the original Greenways café was behind their fish and chip shop, which was entered by another door at the side front. The shop was close to the original market and cattle market entrance, all demolished to build the Brunel centre and Sainsbury's.

Greenways was a favourite haunt of the bikers, all the motor bikes lined up in front of the fish and chip shop. The café had a juke box and pinball machine. From the 1950s, until Mokaris café opened in the early 60s, Greenways was the only teenage type café. Most teenagers who frequented it dressed in Rocker style. The Mods tended to go to Mokaris when that style came in.

The new Greenways moved to the bottom end towards Sainsbury's when the Brunel centre was opened. I have lots of memories from the old town, good days in a much more sociable place back then. (Oh by the way, the tea was awful, stewed putting it politely.)

Kathleen Roberts

I remember the original Greenways. It used to cost sixpence for a portion of chips.

Pat Martin

I worked at the original Greenways part time after school, peeling the potatoes and chipping them for the chip shop. I did it for the two ladies who worked in the café as well, when they asked me on the qt. They used to give me half a crown for doing it for them.

Ken Dobson

My Aunt Pearl worked in the café. Maybe she was one of those ladies.

Gwen Garrett

I have wonderful memories of that café, spent many an hour in there with our friends. Bikers from all over were always there. You could always get a lift anywhere on one of the bikes, usually to the cafe in Little Brickhill if Greenways was a bit quiet.

The café had wonderful cheese crusty rolls - and if we played truant and went in there, no one asked you why you weren't at school! Great times.

Rosemary Sellars

I remember my mum having fish and chips with a bunch of Hell's Angels in the café. They were decent guys and even bought my mum a cake for her afters! Great days, sorely missed.

Paul Bird

As teenagers, Greenways was where everyone met before going to Wilton Hall, or just to meet up. If you were looking for a mate you would find them there. Wonderful memories.

Janice Gibbison

THE NEWFOUNDOUT

The Newfoundout is just outside what is now the Blue Lagoon Nature Reserve, which officially opened in 1994.

Jean Blane Flannery

The Newfoundout, with Water Eaton Road at the end of the path and Bletchley station on the horizon.

That path brings back horrible memories of cross country running at Bletchley Grammar School.

Nick Halewood

Round there was our cross country course! Sometimes the weather was atrocious.

Glyn Ottery

I will always remember it as a great fossil hunting area where ammonites could be prised from the clay nearest to the water.

Simon Valledy

My strongest memory is of collecting bullrushes - and getting wet feet. Mum had a really tall vase she used for them (the bullrushes, not wet feet!)

Jean Blane Flannery

BLETCHLEY AND FENNY TAPESTRY OF THOUGHTS

We always used to get bulrushes from the blue lagoon.
Vernon Leslie Howe

My mum used to love the bullrushes too.

I went down there fishing for sticklebacks with a net, with my grandad Blane. And yes I got wet feet too.
Christine Barlow

I used to collect bull rushes too and yes, got wet muddy feet.
Janice Gibson

Yeah, not sure what the fascination with the rushes was!
Wendy Hook

The things we used to do with no health and safety restrictions. We just had good times with friends in mud and muck, with no hand gel etc. And we got through.
Pam Tew

I remember too, but Mum sadly went past it today - no access.
Anne Falcus

MANOR FIELDS SPORTS GROUND

Manor Fields Sports ground was officially opened by the Duke of Edinburgh 14 October 1952, with the unveiling of a plaque.

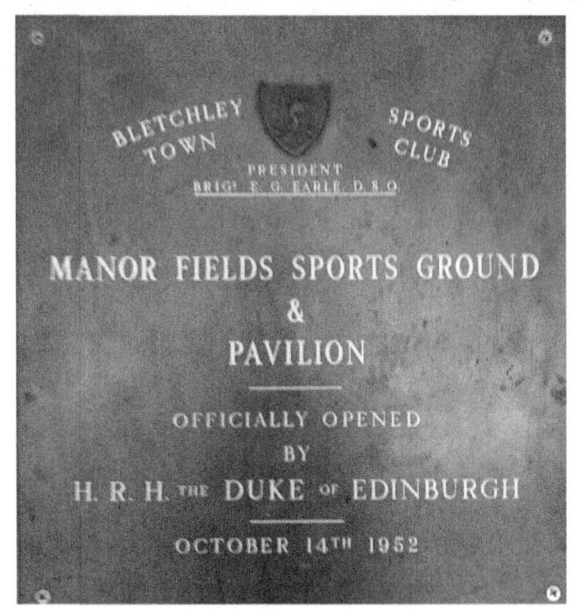

BLETCHLEY TOWN SPORTS CLUB
PRESIDENT
BRIG^r F. G. EARLE D.S.O.

MANOR FIELDS SPORTS GROUND
&
PAVILION

OFFICIALLY OPENED
BY
H. R. H. THE DUKE OF EDINBURGH

OCTOBER 14TH 1952

Prior to unveiling the plaque the duke walked through the crowds lining his way and spoke to some of the local rugby players.

Among the children who stood waiting to greet him and cheer when he arrived were the Girls Life Brigade Cadets, me among them. The trouble was, a boil had just come up on the back of my right knee. The duke was two hours late getting to us and I was in agony by the time the event was over. I had to walk home - no mobiles to use to ask for help and no phone at home anyway.

When I got to Victoria Road I was able to stop for a rest. My Aunt Margaret Blane was working in the Co-op there and found a chair for me to sit on. I eventually got home and when Dad came in from work he took me on the crossbar of his bike down to the evening Surgery. The doctor lanced the boil. That day is a really painful memory - as you might imagine.

I was of course in any event too young to attend the dance held in the pavilion on the opening evening.

Jean Blane Flannery

Thanks to Kathleen Bairstow for this photo of the evening.

THE STUDIO

A key thread to be woven into our Tapestry of Thoughts is the Studio. This iconic building opened its doors 5 October 1936, showing "Mr Deeds goes to Town" starring Gary Cooper.

Many members will remember visits to the Studio as a child. Others will remember their courting days, while some will remember taking their own children there.

It was a very big part of growing up in Bletchley for me as my granny Peggy Basketfield worked there for 38 years, starting in 1946. Her first job was to stoke up the boiler with coke, keeping the cinema fires burning and the cinema heated.

She also cycled around all the villages, sticking huge posters on bill boards to advertise forthcoming films. From that she moved to cleaning, to working as an usherette, and often also Front of House as cashier.

15 August 1980 the projection equipment was modernised., the then manager Lionel Walters.

Despite such efforts at modernisation the Studio was forced to close 9 December 1986, with the final film being "Alien" starring Sigorney Weaver. The manager at the time was Phil South.

I hope through this story to pay tribute to the many workers from the Studio that did a great job in the local community.

Diane McLean

I had 2 sisters who worked at the Studio as usherettes, Ann and Iris.

As teenagers, we frequented the Studio at least twice a week. The back row was always taken by couples, so they could cuddle up.

I had my first and last puff on a cigarette in the front row. About 4 or 5 of us from Saffron Street were together. I think one of the boys lit up a cigarette and passed it along. We were still at school but I can't remember how young.

We also used to go and see "A" rated films, which unaccompanied children were not allowed to watch. It was not unusual for us to stand outside and ask an adult who was going in to buy us a ticket, for which we paid them. I can't imagine that ever happening in today's world. Life then seemed so innocent.

Kathleen Bairstow

My mother worked as an usherette with " Scotch Peg" as she always called her.

Malcolm Wheeler

Captioned "Peggy playing one of her familiar roles."

I went to see Monty Python's "Meaning of Life" with my girlfriend on the same night as the Milton Keynes Central's fireworks show.

We were the only paying customers for that performance. We had the whole place to ourselves but the lady with the ice cream tray still did the walk down the aisle.

Jerry Roberts

I remember the bomb scare when we were starting to watch "Star Wars." The studio was evacuated.

Its closure was such a great loss for Bletchley. It was a very sad day standing on the multi-story carpark, watching part of my childhood memories being demolished.

Vernon Leslie Howe

THE COUNTY

The County Cinema on Fenny high Street went through a number of incarnations. The building was originally a Methodist Chapel. It was converted into a cinema, the Palace, which opened 16 October 1911 with "The Leading Lady." The cinema could initially seat 514 people.

County Cinemas chain took it over in 1927 and re-named it the Majestic. It was renovated and renamed King George's Cinema in 1929. In 1932 it was renamed County Cinema, its last incarnation.

Jean Blane Flannery

My granny worked at the County before starting at the Studio. My dad used to tell how each visit he'd leave his balaclava under the seat - but somehow it always managed to find its way back to him.

Diane McLean

"Saturday Morning Pictures" was a weekly ritual while I lived in Western Road and even later. It cost sixpence and was great value for money with a cartoon, a serial and a feature film every week. The serial always left you with a cliffhanger - but the hero wasn't in nearly so much trouble at the start of the next episode!

Jean Blane Flannery

The narrow pavement along the A5 was quite scary, though luckily not the amount of traffic there is now. Saturday morning pictures was a real bargain for 6d. I never went on the balcony as that was 9d. Good memories.

Janice Gibbison

I went to the County a few times. My Gran lived opposite the alleyway at the side of cinema. She lived at 28 Church Street many years ago.

Margaret McCracken Hogg

I remember Mr Betteridge the manager letting us out row by row at the end of Saturday morning pictures.

Jeff Dolling

All I remember of the County was going to see Calamity Jane when I was 8 and Buck Rogers on Saturday mornings.

Christine Chapman

I loved Saturday morning pictures. If I had enough money, we would go upstairs in the 9d end.

Barry Linford

I went there a couple of times to kids' Saturday morning pictures. My mother-in-law used to work there.

Robert Evans

The first photo is of the original church, with its narrow pavement. The second shows the County's sorry state on demolition.

The County sadly closed its doors for the last time 29 June 1957, with James Robertson Justice and Dirk Bogarde in "Doctor At Large."

Jean Blane Flannery

MEAGER'S HILL

Meager's Hill on Buckingham Road takes its name from the Meager (pronounced Major) family.

Tom Meager established a forge at the top of the hill opposite The Grange in the late nineteenth century and the family lived in an old cottage nearby, also owning a large tract of land with an extensive orchard.

Meager's Hill looking towards Buckingham, taken in the early 20th century before a paved road was built by the family in 1922.

In the 1960s the family sold off parcels of land for housing development, hence Orchard Close halfway up the hill.

In 1946, John Meager was one of my late mother's sponsors when she came to the UK from The Netherlands in order to marry my father in March 1946. Her other sponsor was Bob Blane (of Bletchley Co-op).

Although John and his wife Mollie had 3 children, they were the last occupants of the cottage and are now both deceased.

John Goss

LOCAL SCHOOLS

BLETCHLEY ROAD SCHOOL

Bletchley Road School is a place steeped in history with many stories to tell of sporting achievements and other varied curriculum activities through the journey of time.

The school had a role to play during the second World War. Many evacuees spent their time there, along with teachers from the Islington area of London.

It is a school that has had many name changes over the decades and opened as Leon Comprehensive School in 1973.

it was during that year that Leon secondary pupils moved from Bletchley Road to Fern Grove on the Lakes estate. Also in 1973,

Bletchley Grammar School and Wilton School amalgamated to become Lord Grey School.

So from 1973 Bletchley had only two secondary schools. One was in Rickley Lane and one on The Lakes estate. And the stigma of the 11+ ended.

Knowles School reopened on the site of Bletchley Road School and by 1973 was fully operational as a junior school.

Diane McLean

Bletchley Road School was the grounding for the people we became! War time struggles, school maybe not as exciting as we thought it should be, but we are a generation of British bulldogs. Throw anything at us and we will use it to our advantage.

I am sad at what has happened to dear old Bletchley, but proud to have been a part of the best part.

Gwen Garrett

Ken Barnwell looking cool "back in the day," joining the other Bletchley Road Boys.

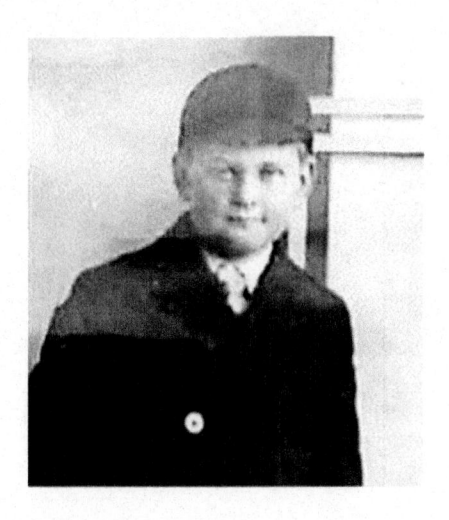

Ken affectionately referred to the school as "Barrel Cook's School for Backward Boys." My dad, an old mate of Ken's, would have loved that.

Dad hated school, preferring to spend his days with his Uncle Jim Goodman at the allotments. When he did get hoiked back by the truancy guy - who apparently did the rounds on his bike - it would be for a caning from Barrel Cook.

Diane McLean

Barrel Cook was a little rotund man. He stood on the edge of the stage at morning assembly while we sat on the floor. He was north country and used to say every morning, "I don't speak to people who don't loooook at me." He looked so wobbly I used to think he was going to fall over.

Marie Love

This photo is of Bletchley Road Junior School, with Mr Snaith at the helm - a wonderful memory from the early 1960s.

Enlarging the photo enabled me to track down Ann Elliott standing next to Candy May.

My face is practically obscured by the huge bow the girl standing in front of me has in her hair! The culprit I believe is Susan Goose!

Ann Elliott Stephens

Here is the Bletchley Road Junior School athletics team after winning at the Wolverton Sports Ground in 1956 or 1957 and taken in Leon Rec' with the school behind.

Teachers: Miss Fitton, Head Mr Snaith and Mr Burns.

Diane McLean

John Roberts

John as a boy   John in later years

I feel very privileged to have met John Roberts and his beautiful wife Kathleen, a lovely local couple who both attended Bletchley Road School.

Earlier this year John, whom Kathleen describes as her Prince Charming, celebrated his 90th birthday with family and friends.

John like my grandad Albert Basketfield, worked at Wolverton Works. "Back in the day" this was a source of local employment for very many.

John was in the same class at Bletchley Road School as my mum Joyce Farmer née Basketfield, sharing the same teachers and friends. Kathleen lovingly shares John's memories of his schooldays.

Diane McLean

John started at Bletchley Road School in 1944 and left in 1948, aged 15 years. During his time at the school Barrel Cook was headmaster.

John remembers getting the cane on a couple of occasions. One time he was sent to the headmaster by Mr Puryer for cracking a new sheet of plastic, which he had been specifically warned to be careful with. He was using the plastic to make a set of salad servers. On another occasion he was caned for giving cheek to Mrs Linnelle.

Bletchley Road School had a reputation for being very strict, and indeed it was. The cane was a punishment given quite freely to both boys and girls. Certain areas of the grounds were out of bounds during breaks and lunchtimes. Boys and girls had their own separate playgrounds, and woe betide anyone caught out in the wrong place without permission.

The school also had strong traditions. However, during the war years Speech Days weren't held. This was a great shame, as after the class exams the top boy and girl would each be awarded a prize.

These prizes were presented to them by the honoured guest speaker, usually a local dignitary, at the Speech Day. (I was a recipient in 1962.) Christmas parties were still held and John remembers his great embarrassment on being singled out to dance with his then form teacher, Mrs Hamilton.

Mostly the teachers were firm but fair, and they were proud of their well-behaved pupils. It would also be fair to say that the pupils took a pride in being part of the school and made lifelong friends during their time there.

Kathleen Roberts

BLETCHLEY ROAD INFANTS SCHOOL

School House and Infants School

My younger sister Carole was very unhappy in her one term at Bletchley Road Infants School. Although she did feel overwhelmed, the main reason was that she couldn't stand the toilets! She said they were dirty and smelly - and she wouldn't use them.

It's a good job we went home for dinner or I shudder to think what might have happened. As it was, at playtime she was always at the railings between the infant and junior schools looking for me. I wanted to play with my friends but couldn't leave her standing there, upset and almost in tears.

Fortunately for her, we moved to Stewartby after that term. She was happy at the nice small school - with its lovely clean toilets.

Although I found Bletchley Juniors noisy and busy after Church Green Road, I hadn't wanted to leave Bletchley and I know Mum hadn't. She loved Bletchley and living close to her sister Nellie Cutts. But Dad felt he had no career prospects at Bletchley Works and accepted a promotion to Stewartby as Club Secretary.

Jean Blane Flannery

BLETCHLEY ROAD AND WATER EATON SCHOOLS: WILLIAM CRISP

Remembering the late Mr William Crisp - a well-known, much loved and highly respected member of the local community.

William Crisp began his teaching career in North London in the 1920s. From there he moved to Smethwick - working in a school for deprived boys. In 1935 he moved to Buckinghamshire and took up the position of headmaster at Stewkley School, moving within three years to Bletchley Road Junior School.

Following the outbreak of war, William became a member of the welcoming party that greeted the first train of evacuees from London in 1939 and he was appointed as Deputy Billeting Officer.

William Crisp was a genial, exuberant and very innovative teacher. It was in 1953 that he was appointed to the headship of the new Water Eaton School. He was a distinguished character who is affectionately remembered by those whose lives he touched in a career that spanned four decades.

Diane McLean

Water Eaton School netball team with Miss Gilbert and Mr Crisp
Back L-R Christine Walters, Francesca Henderson, Tina Farmer
Front L-R Linda Lewis, Judy Crawford, Christine Oxford, Barbara Panter, Gina Lewis

Mr Crisp invited back to Bletchley Grammar School for Speech Day

WILTON SCHOOL

Wilton School opened in September 1955.

First year of Wilton School. After this year a few of us went on to Wolverton Tech.

After my first senior school year, when I attended Bletchley Road Secondary School, a new school was opened nearer to the Saints estate in Bletchley.

It was to be called Wilton School and was situated in the RAF grounds in Rickley Lane. The school was very modern with large expanses of windows, which made the classrooms bright and airy.

I mated up with a lad called Richard Spanner, who had moved to Bletchley from Peckham. Luckily Richard and I both passed the 13+ exams and went to Wolverton Tech together.

We have remained friends since those days, as have Terry Foster and a few others. Sadly our numbers have declined due to our age and Covid has seriously hampered our attempts to meet regularly again.

It was a journey of many paths meeting in those early days of 1955/56, with all our stories of how we came together, and I suppose it is only right that the centre of the hub of our crew is Terry, the local lad. I still remember some of the discussions relating to what our future hopes in life were.

Teachers I remember were Tug Wilson, Bubby Harris, Mr Held and Mr Bennett. Our form teacher was Mr Garrett, whose favourite way of attracting someone's attention was with his four rulers held together with elastic bands landing on or near your shoulder or nape of your neck!

I enjoyed sport and PT, without excelling at any of it. I was hampered by a slipped disc in my back, the result of a playground accident where I slipped on ice.

This necessitated me having to wear a rather wide and uncomfortable "plaster of paris" belt for five months, extremely hot and uncomfortable in the summer.

It wasn't long before Richard found a use for it! He would dare a lad to elbow me in the stomach as hard as he could - in return for one of Richard's elbows on his opponent.

Another trick of Richard's was - after eating a curry at our house - borrowing a chilli from my mum and telling other pupils it was an Indian sweet. Thank goodness my mum only used mild ones! No one was hurt by these pranks, unlike some of the "vicious" conker games that went on.

School was never a chore to me and even though I was more interested in Maths and Science, I also liked History and

Geography. But Art held no fascination and I'm still at matchstick figure level.

As a youngster I had extremely sweaty hands and my exercise books were never the neatest or the tidiest specimens in the class, but this condition did rectify itself as the years passed.

I spent a lot of time with mates playing football and cricket in the fields between Church Green Road and Buckingham Road, behind Keys Shop. If we had enough cash we'd go for a round of pitch and putt at Central Gardens, which if memory serves me right cost us fourpence each.

In later years we would cycle towards Bedford or Northampton and do a bit of train spotting at any convenient bridge over a railway track.

The year at Wilton passed and we were looking forward to the next year until one day near the end of the final term. As Catholics, for some reason we had to wait in a classroom while assembly was held. But this day we were brought in after the assembly finished for an announcement of who had passed the 13+ and would be going to Wolverton Tech.

Above from left in 1956 Johnny, Heather, Linda (Mary), Robert.

They all followed me to Wilton as the school evolved.

William McLaughlin

The French Teacher

While I was at Wilton School a Frenchman was employed as its French Language teacher. He certainly brought a new and different style to the classroom, with assembled Airfix planes suspended from his classroom lights (I think he made them but I might be wrong).

Having a tall Frenchman who insisted on speaking and writing only French was so out of the box for the time. With tempting bombers hanging on cotton threads from lights, his classes turned into noisy, active fiascos.

In typical French well-dressed style, his tan coloured woollen fitted jacket, impeccable white shirt and light trousers sadly became the target of ink flicked from well filled fountain pens.

Elastic bands catapulted tightly folded wads of notebook paper, which zoomed like weapons of mass destruction, hitting the unsuspecting teacher or the aircraft. When hit, bits of the aircraft fell to the floor.

A French class it was not. A war zone it was.

I shamefully admit to having enjoyed the fun at the beginning, but after a while I found seeing the state of our teacher's clothing and classroom a total embarrassment.

This new venture by Wilton School was a very early attempt to encourage Brits to learn other languages. However, the attempt was unsuccessful - the unfortunate Frenchman's stay short lived and unappreciated.

Judith Kutty

BLETCHLEY GRAMMAR SCHOOL

We moved to Bletchley in March 1961 and I did a term and a half at Rickley Lane Primary School.

I had taken the eleven plus in London before moving and got the results when in Bletchley. I remember the panic my mother had over having to buy the grammar school uniform.

Luckily my dad had a railway mate whose daughter was at BGS a few years ahead of me and gave me her hand me downs - much to my mother's relief.

I remember those hats. I hated them. You were living dangerously if you dared take yours off to or from the journey to school. But they set us up as sitting targets.

The felt ones turned into pudding bowls when they got wet. Mum kept my straw one for years. My daughter used to play with it when she went round.

Geraldine Cable

A memory from May 1964 - when a letter of acceptance to Bletchley Grammar School landed on our doormat. It could be described as one of life's defining moments.

To my dad it most certainly was, not least for the hours of overtime he put in on the railway to pay for my uniform. He was very proud as I was the only person from our family to have passed the 11+ exam. He himself had spent hours tutoring me with those ghastly brown "progress papers!"

I perhaps did not realise the enormity of his pride until recently when, going through one of his boxes, I found my blazer badge tucked away alongside his Masonic badges and memorabilia - the highest accolade of all, bless him.

Diane McLean

I always remember my mum saying I couldn't open the letter until my dad was home from his railway job.

He cried when it was opened. He was so proud, as was my mum. The years before had been hard for them, arriving from Ireland in the fifties. I'm sure my pass was as much for them as for me and they never stopped supporting me until the day they died.

Their sacrifices were many, just so I could wear that badge.

Teresa Skinner

Our Headmaster at Wavendon Primary, Mr Morgan, tutored 4 of us from our class - 3 boys and me. It obviously helped, as we all passed. But I think we were also all reasonably intelligent, as he had already realised.

My dad was proud too. He gave me £5, which was a lot of money in the 1960s. I loved BGS. But being the only girl from my school was pretty daunting at first!

Mary Church Hazell

Kathleen Fryer

Kathleen Fryer, seen here in 1959 in her role as form tutor at Bletchley Grammar School, taught Art there for many years.

Diane McLean

I have some lovely memories of lovely Miss Fryer. Aka Kate, she taught me well at BGS and I remain proud of my Art 'O' level.

Kate certainly inspired and encouraged me. She sent a small group of us out into the town one afternoon every week, to sketch with pen and ink just what we saw and fancied. These sketches of mine were published in this group a few months ago, after I discovered 50 years later that my late mother had kept them!

However I didn't touch a paintbrush after leaving BGS, to paint a picture at least, until long after I retired so 50 years later. I now have my paintings scattered around the house and my family.

Having got back to painting again now, I have setup the Wootton U3A Art Group here in Northampton. I love it! Well done Kate.

It would be lovely to meet her again, especially as I see she lives not far from me.

Colin Brown

A lesser known fact about Kathleen is that at the age of 15 she inadvertently became a film "artist" during a trip with a friend to Maidenhead.

At Beaconsfield they stopped to watch the shooting of an outdoor scene for a "Just William" film and asked if they could take part. Given a role as extras, they stood at a garden gate pointing at William as he ran past carrying a bunch of flowers, his dog with him.

John Clark, the 13-year-old actor who played William in the BBC series, had opened the Bletchley Company Boys' Brigade fête the previous year. Perhaps that is why they got the role?

Jean Blane Flannery

The Donald Halewood Story

Donald Halewood was born in Liverpool 21 May 1922. Many will remember this lovely man for his role within the local community where he did indeed touch many lives - weaving many storylines that are repeatedly shared by so many of us.

Donald studied at Magdalen College Oxford, his studies interrupted when he joined the Parachute Regiment. He finally finished his MA and began his teaching career in Grimsby before moving to Manchester. His subjects were Classics, English and Humanities.

Donald, his wife Mabel and two young sons, moved to Bletchley in 1956. They lived in Newton Road and Selbourne Avenue where their son Simon was born.

The family finally settled at "White Knights" in Great Brickhill, where Donald was a lay preacher at St Mary's Church.

Many will remember Donald Halewood for his role as headteacher at Bletchley Grammar School. The school opened in 1956, built in what was part of the grounds of Bletchley Park. He remained as head of the school until 1973 when it became a comprehensive, amalgamating with Wilton School to become Lord Grey.

Donald Halewood sadly passed away 27 December 1989, aged 67 years. He really was a man with a story to tell. I am proud to have known him and honoured to write this small snapshot of that story

Thanks go to his eldest son Nick for providing this information.

Diane McLean

LORD GREY SCHOOL

Wilton School and Bletchley Grammar School amalgamated in September 1973 to become Lord Grey School.

Diane McLean

I went to Lord Grey from the grammar school when it first started. I was just going into the fourth year. From what I can remember we still kept in our grammar school classes/houses, Trevithick for me, formerly Cottesloe at BGS. Mostly we had the same teachers as before.

The two sets of pupils tended to stick within their own groups. I remember a bit of rivalry but can't recall anything serious. We did mix in the sports teams where the emphasis was more on football than rugby, which the grammar school had preferred.

I presume that as all the older pupils went through it became more of a united school and things evened themselves out.

Myles Phillips

CHURCH GREEN ROAD (ST MARY'S CHURCH of ENGLAND) SCHOOL

From the school records:

"Tuesday November 26th 1940 - Miss Z. Bailey of Slough was appointed headmistress of Old Bletchley Church of England School and began the next Monday."

Note that here she is called Miss Bailey. In other places later, she is referred to as Mrs Bailey. I should think the formal record is correct but always knew her as Mrs Bailey.

The school had 3 classrooms, each with an old, black, freestanding coke-burning stove near the front (actually quite close to the teacher's desk!) to provide heat for the winter.

One room was for the Infants (five to seven years old), the other 2 for junior school age, eight to eleven. We sat, two to a desk, at old-fashioned (and old) wooden desks with bench seats attached. The desk surfaces were quite uneven, making writing sometimes rather wonky.

Thanks to Pamela Essam for the photo below. Her story follows.

Jean Blane Flannery

Mrs Bailey with a group of schoolchildren outside Pamela's home.

My first school, in 1943, was St Mary's Church of England Infants in Church Green Road.

The school was just across the road from our house. I don't really remember my first day but I will share some memories of my time at the school when the headmistress was Mrs Zilpah Bailey.

Mrs Bailey was a friend of my parents and I remember her visiting our house.

My class teacher was Miss Gascoine. My friends who I played with and grew up with were Josie Meredith, Edythe Stevens, Joyce and Freda Healey and Maureen Cursley.

Mrs Bailey would ask for volunteers to go round to her house to listen for the phone or to take her washing to a lady in Grange Road. My hand was always one of the first to go up.

Miss Gascoine did not like us going to the toilet in class time. This was a bit hard on us as we were only 5 years old.

I wet my knickers one day and she asked me to explain why my chair was wet. I replied that the girl sitting next to me (Josie Meredith) had wet herself and it had come all over my chair.

I wore shoes that had a strap over with a small button. The button came off one day and when I arrived home to tell my mum, she asked me what I had done with it. As I did not have a pocket, I said it was up my nose. Luckily a nurse lived nearby and she was able to get it down.

We had to go to church one morning a week on a Thursday. So a long line of children all holding hands could always be seen walking down the road on that day.

When we got to the age of about 7 or 8 years, some pupils had to go to overspill classes at the Yeomanry Hall in Newton Road. Mrs Cutler was the teacher. Her husband was a major in the army and the cane she carried was one of his. I don't remember it being used much.

On the way to this school we had to pass a group of men repairing the road or path. They were Italian prisoners of war. They made us whistles out of reeds.

Mum was a caretaker for the school in Church Green Road for quite a few years.

Church Green Road School Children's Christmas Party
Pamela Essam

Pam is on the right of the first photo, with her sister Eileen. This looks to be about the time she would have been at Church Green Road School. The other photo, of Pam with Eileen and their mother, is one that her father always kept close to him. He carried it in his pocket wherever he went.

Jean Blane Flannery

There used to be a big pile of coal (or coke) in the playground for the fires. We were milk monitors and in the winter used to bring the frozen milk bottles in to thaw by the big fires. Then it looked curdled.

The toilets were outside in a small block round the back and there was a rec just by. We used to go there most days after school. Memories.

Pam Tew

At morning break each child had a free third-pint bottle of milk, with a paper straw. The bottle tops were cardboard,. They had a perforated centre to push out and make a hole for the straw.

With the bottles sitting outside in crates, when the weather was really cold the milk would expand and push the tops up above the rims of the bottles.

The teachers brought in the crates to sit by the stoves, where we could watch the tops slowly sink down. I really liked the milk with flakes of ice in it.

In the nice weather we had nature walks, looking for plant and animal life. We took anything special, or the subject of a lesson, back to school to be placed on the Nature Table at one side of the classroom with our own finds.

Jean Blane Flannery

I remember the toilets and the rec. Lots of times in the summer our mums from Newton Road would meet us after school and we would play and have a picnic. My granny would come up too sometimes, from Buckingham Road. Happy Days

Diane McLean

Being allowed to play in the rec after school was a big treat. My mum used to come and collect me most days so she would wait while I had a go on the swings or roundabout, or some long rocking thing that they put in later.

Sometimes I used to walk home alone to Park Gardens. I can only have been 6 or 7 and I doubt children would do that these days.

Hilary Smith

I remember my first playtime there. I remember Mrs Bailey, Mrs Littlewood, and Mrs Duncan. Mrs Duncan used to shout and frightened me

Ann Cornish

Mrs Duncan scared me too, so loud !! I remember Mrs Bailey, she always wore a brown suit!!!

Pam Tew

I must have started there in 1958. Dolly Duncan scared everybody. After about one week at the school I was confronted with the real world. My mum had put a KitKat into my jacket pocket for the break. My jacket hung in the cloakroom.

I came out to get the KitKat and found that somebody had stolen half of it. For some reason they left one half. I didn't know what to do, so just swallowed the problem and didn't tell my mum. I just got on with enjoying the school.

Ian Gardner

Mrs Littlewood was head when I went there.

After I went to Holne Chase my mother became secretary at Church Green Road, then a teaching assistant, so I knew all the staff until we moved away in 1973. Mrs Littlewood moved to be head of the new Holne Chase infant school in 1966.

Every time I see the tall hedge around the old school I think of those days - the odd shaped playground, the climbing frame they didn't like us using, and the toilets in the playground, not to mention the coal heaters and the blackboards on easels. Elf and Safety would have a fit!

Richard Pringle

My mum was a teacher there in the 60s. I used to go in sometimes to help out before school returned. It was a lively little school.

Allison Barnett

Who would recognise this building now? Perhaps the name of the house would give it away.

TO AND FROM SCHOOL

Many of us may remember the days of the Lollipop Man or Lady who helped us safely across the road in all weathers, togged up in their waterproof high visibility coats and caps.

My favourite story is of Mr West - the loveliest man, who helped us cross the Buckingham Road outside Chandlers Store.

This very jovial, very kind man helped us safely on our way to Church Green Road and Holne Chase School for many years.

He always seemed to have a never ending supply of sweets in his very deep pockets. Sadly I have no photo of Mr West - but his memory lingers on.

Bletchley Road School of course also had its crossing Lollipop Man. Many of you may remember when Josh Kelly's was the friendly face that ushered you safely across the road.

Diane McLean

Safely crossing from Bletchley Road School

I think my dad may have taken me to my first morning at school, on my 5th birthday in 1949. After that, I and some other children from Whiteley Crescent and Newton Road walked to school on our own.

We went down Newton Road, across the Buckingham Road at the crossroads by the Shoulder of Mutton. There was nobody to help us across the road in those days but there was very little traffic. Sonn after crossing the road we turned right into a little lane, which led us into Church Green Road near the school.

In Spring we picked young hawthorn leaves to eat on the way to school, calling them "bread and cheese." I don't know why, as they didn't taste anything like it. In summer we broke off cow parsley stems to for peashooters, the "peas" being the seeds of the same plant. In late summer we picked and ate blackberries, staining our mouths and fingers.

Wild roses (dog roses) grew in every hedgerow, giving a display of brilliant red rosehips in the autumn. Autumn also brought bright orange Chinese lanterns, which we would pick and carry, pretending they were real lanterns.

On really cold, frosty winter mornings we slid on the ice until it was like glass. When it snowed, we were as excited as children now and we had fun throwing snowballs as we went to and from school.

Cutting through another lane from school brought us out near Key's shop on Buckingham Road. My friend Sandra and I started taking that way home in summer, and went across the road to Holne Chase. There was a pond in the spinney with planks across it that was fun. We were only going to play for a little while...

Dinner time came. I wasn't back when Dad arrived home for dinner on his bicycle and Mum had to tell him. He came to find me and I got told off good and proper but I didn't learn. Eventually I was spanked, for the one and only time. That did no good. What did?

Dad not coming for me, then making me stay in my bedroom for the afternoon when I finally did arrive. And I had to take a note to Mrs Bailey next morning. I didn't know Dad had already spoken to her! But that cured me.

Jean Blane Flannery

I walked home from school at mid-day. Mum always had lunch ("dinner" then) ready. I used to run down Church Green Road with Adrian Hall and Robert Hope until we were stopped by the policeman who controlled the crossing by the Shoulder of Mutton.

"Wait there." Traffic (what there was) halted. Then we were allowed to cross the road. Where Tesco is now was once a farmhouse and an orchard. I used to scrump there!

John Goss

YOUTH GROUPS

BLETCHLEY YOUTH CLUB

There were a number of local youth clubs. One was the Bletchley Youth Club in Derwent Drive. This youth club, unlike so many others, has stood the test of time. It remains open and is still offering a host of activities to the youth of today.

The legendary Barrie Field worked tirelessly in his role as youth club leader to make this venture a huge success. He used his contacts to set up bands that performed at the venue. He organised trips that are still vivid in many memories to this day.

So let's hear it for Barrie Field and his contributions to the local community.

Diane McLean

I can remember taking Manfred Mann down to the "Chinky" in town in my old Austin A35, my first motor, before they played at Derwent Drive.'

Bryan Payne

SALVATION ARMY YOUNG PEOPLE

We used to go to The Salvation Army in Church St, Fenny Stratford.

This photo was taken at the yearly Book Presentation Service.

My brother Alan is top row 2nd from the right, my brother Michael 2nd in from the left middle row, and little old me 5th one in from the right on the bottom row.

I would think I was about 5 years old so this would have been 1955.
Sheila Batham

Joe McLelland in the centre - known to children as 'Uncle Joe' - was the Young People's Sergeant Major.
Douglas Sellers

Spent many an hour in Central Gardens: sitting, playing, listening to the Salvation Army Band play in there, eventually playing my tambourine in the band, so many memories.
Sheila Batham

THE FREEMAN MEMORIAL METHODIST CHURCH YOUTH CLUB

The youth club photographed in the Albert Street Church, late 1940s. Centre is Stuart Robinson (Robbie) leader for many years.

This youth club began in 1944. It is indeed a group with a lot of local history. Early leadership was led by Stuart Robinson (Robbie), assisted by Phyllis Baker and Janet Ebbs.

As time went by, weekly meetings were held in the building at the back of the church. Leaders that many members of this group will remember are David Ebbs, Ken Breedon and Stan Fullman.

In the late sixties I was a committee member, along with Arthur Pember and Gisella Perry. We would take it in turns to host meetings - thanks to our long suffering parents.

The youth group was active. We took part in sponsored walks, regular trips were organised and we would attend youth conventions - on one occasion winning first prize for a drama production that was written and produced In House.

Diane McLean

Robbie I remember as a lovely, kind and jovial man, Clerk of the County Court. His two sons, Ian and Hugh were good pals of mine and I went through Holne Chase, and grammar school with Ian.

Colin Brown

Blimey, a blast from the past! Freeman Church and the youth club were major features in my life in Bletchley. My parents were staunch Methodists and we never failed to be at church every Sunday.

Mum and Dad would spend hours chatting to folk after the morning services so my sisters and I would sit in Dad's car and listen to Tony Blackburn on Radio London (pop pirate station) doing his chart show. My mum ran the junior choir and we'd put on productions occasionally in the hall, as well as singing in church.

The youth club went on camping expeditions for a few years, in May I think. I remember going to a farm in Nash a couple of times and camping by the side of the river in Gayhurst. This would've been 1967-1969ish. Ray Gauthier took his canoe to Gayhurst and we took it in turns to paddle down the river. The gatehouse to Gayhurst Manor was still a pub then. I think it was called the Francis Drake and it was just across the road from the river - very convenient!

My sister Ally and I would regularly adjourn to The George after youth club on Fridays. I had my first pint there.

Peter Lubbock

GIRL GUIDES

My mother Joyce Farmer née Basketfield was born in Eaton Avenue in 1933, growing up in wartime Bletchley. Mum has seen many changes to her beloved home town during her lifetime.

A recent conversation with her 12 year old granddaughter, who is a Girl Guide, prompted Mum's story.

11 November 1946 Mum was chosen from the Bletchley and Fenny Girl Guide unit to lay a wreath at the war memorial in Bletchley Road. It was an honour that she is proud of to this day.

The captain of the unit was Miss Munday. The lieutenant was Roberta Pickard, who can be seen here on her wedding day.

Roberta married John Tolton and the Guides formed a guard of honour for them. I am sure it was a very moving sight to behold.

The Guide unit was linked to the Methodist Church in Bletchley, the minister at that time Mr Holdsworthy.

The Guides worked closely with the Scouts on Parade Days.

This photo is of a May Day Parade. Mum remembers them all marching along Bletchley Road in the pouring rain, getting soaked to the skin.

The Guides met in the Co-op Hall in Albert Street and had to pay a small weekly fee. The uniform cost £1 - which seems quite steep for those days.

Camping trips were all part of the fun of being a Girl Guide.

Activities were interesting and varied just as I am sure they are today. A favourite activity was "tracking"- arrows were placed along a route that led the Guides to a destination where a learning experience would take place.

On one such expedition they were led to a phone box and taught how to make a phone call.

I wonder what today's activity was to be

On another occasion they were taught morse code and Mum remembers getting into trouble at home for tapping messages through the bedroom wall to her next door neighbour and friend, Hilda Cook.

Of the 12 girls in the unit, Mum can remember Margaret Basketfield (her younger sister), Judy Blogg, Davina Buckingham, Marjorie Burnett, Margaret Clements, Hilda Cook, Margaret Healey (her best friend), Audrey Lines and Mavis Tunks.

Happy memories of Girl Guiding have lasted a lifetime.

Diane McLean

THE SPURGEON MEMORIAL BAPTIST CHURCH BOYS' BRIGADE

Many young Bletchley boys were member of the Boys' Brigade, my cousin Ken Cutts and our friend Terry Foster being two of them.

As with all the young people's groups, they met weekly and they also had trips to annual camps. Some years they went to Llandudno and the following photo was taken at Bletchley Station as they prepared to leave on one such trip.

Jean Blane Flannery

North Bucks Times, Thursday 1 August 1957.
The Bletchley Boys' Brigade go camping.
On the down fast platform, Platform 3, of Bletchley station.

Standing: Brian Miller, Rod Parker, Ron Bates, Ian Wilson, Pete Gates, Bernie Hill, Roger Ivory
Seated Left to Right: Ken Cutts, Jeff Dolling, Pete Circuit, Bob Burdett, Rodney Toms, Malcolm Webb, Me, Alan Christie, Alf Lucas, Colin Pavey, Pete Burdett, Ian Javes, Dave Philips

Terry Foster

This was before my time in the Boys' Brigade but it was probably the last time of boys going to camp in full uniform because grey windcheaters were later introduced as "camp uniform."

Douglas Sellers

I remember going to the camp at Llandudno, think it was 1968. I was in the 3rd Bletchley.

Andrew Brown

2nd Bletchley Boys' Brigade 1961, photo courtesy Arthur Pember

Photo courtesy Malcolm Wheeler

CALL THE DOCTOR

Very few people had their own phones when I was young. If you needed the doctor urgently you called from the nearest public phone box, which wouldn't be far away. Those were the days too when all GPs made house calls and knew every patient personally.

If you had a less urgent medical problem, you just went down to the surgery and sat in the waiting room until the doctor called you in. There was no appointment system.

I was born in my aunt and uncle's house in Cambridge Street and it was I think Dr Madison who came to the house to deliver me. That was a few years before the NHS was created in July 1948, soon after we had moved to Whiteley Crescent. Until then, all patients had to pay the doctor themselves unless they were "charity cases."

For some years as a child I was quite sickly, as they used to say. I had bouts of tonsillitis until I had my tonsils out and, in the winter months particularly, bronchitis as well.

I remember Dr Lufkin coming out to me quite a number of times after we moved to Whiteley Crescent. She prescribed penicillin medicine, which was quite new at the time. I hated it. It was thick, pink and supposedly raspberry tasting - ugh! I tried to hide under the piano stool when I heard the doctor arrive. (It didn't work...)

My sister Carole was born in Whiteley Crescent, in the early hours of a February Sunday in 1949. Dr Lufkin delivered her and Dad brought Carole into my bedroom to show me our new baby. I knew that Dr Lufkin had been and thought that she had brought the baby with her in her big black bag. I was four years old.

Jean Blane Flannery

Doctors Gleave, Hobbs and Jarvis were the doctors in their surgery in Bletchley Road when I was little. They had 1 little waiting room and 1 surgery. There was no reception and there were no nurses. You just used to sit in the waiting room and wait for your turn.

That little building is still in Bletchley Road and I always glance over to it when we go by in the car. Although it's now Queensway, to me it will always be Bletchley Road.

Sheila Batham

Dr Clements was our family doctor for years, either at his Shenley road surgery or for home visits at Shenley Brook End. He was stern, no messing, but he was respected by my dad who did his best to avoid doctors.

Dr Clements virtually saved my dad's life when he had a twisted gut (intussusception), as father for several hours wouldn't allow us to go the telephone box to call. Dr Clements also delivered (breach birth) my little sister at home.

After many years he came on a house call and met both my own little boys!

Judith Kutty

Old Dr Morphy (Brian's dad) came to see me in the summer holidays every day when I had the measles. Every time he came he left me a penny and the pile of pennies grew bigger on the mantelpiece on the bedroom. He was a lovely man with a lovely Scottish accent.

Ann Cornish

I remember going to see Dr Madison at the surgery behind Ashley Yorke hair salon and the smell from the salon was, and still is, a reminder of walking down the alley towards the surgery.

Teresa Sinclair

We had Dr Gleave from Bletchley Road back in the late 1950s-early 60s. He always came out to us when we had our childhood illnesses. I think when he retired Dr Jarvis took over. I can still remember sitting in that waiting room waiting our turn to be called in. I believe that's where our mums met when they were expecting us, Trudy Haycock.

Karen Leggett nee Watkins

DOCTOR IN THE FRONT LINE

NEWS comes through from Dr. Barnard Maddison, that he was landed in Normandy with a medical unit on "D" Day, and is now in the front line.

The greetings of his many Bletchley friends will go out to him, as they wish for him a speedy return.

Gazette cutting

COMMEMORATION

FENNY POPPERS

Aylesbury Street and St. Martin's Church:

Both are "never ending stories" that we never tire of. I am throwing the Fenny Poppers into the mix because "You can't have one without the other."

The Poppers date back in time to 1724, when Lord of the Manor Browne Willis purchased the land on 11 November that very year - the year the foundation stone for the new church was laid. If you wondered how the event came about its name.

Browne Willis' grandfather Thomas, a notable physician, died in St Martin's Lane in St Martin-in-the-Fields, London, 11 November 1675. By coincidence, this is the feast day of St Martin of Tours.

The Poppers are fired 3 times on St Martin's Day - 11th November. They date back in time to 1724 but no record exists of their first use. There is of course no connection to Remembrance Day.

In history notable dates are:
1901 fired to mourn the death of Queen Victoria
1 January 2000 at 11am to mark the beginning of a new millennium
4 August 2000 at 2pm for the 100th birthday of the Queen Mother

Custodian of the Fenny Poppers is Mr Peter G White, whom I am proud to have met and had the opportunity to talk to. I am embarrassed to say that he was taken aback to learn that in my 69 years of living in Bletchley the first time I had heard or seen them fired was on that very day.

Diane McLean

Having lived in Fenny Stratford for over 42 years, today I had the honour of firing one of the fenny poppers. As I was behind the popper I unfortunately have no photo but I was presented with this certificate.

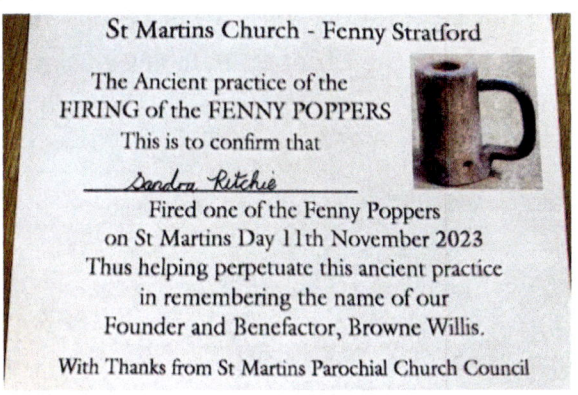

> **St Martins Church - Fenny Stratford**
>
> The Ancient practice of the
> FIRING of the FENNY POPPERS
> This is to confirm that
>
> _Sandra Ritchie_
>
> Fired one of the Fenny Poppers
> on St Martins Day 11th November 2023
> Thus helping perpetuate this ancient practice
> in remembering the name of our
> Founder and Benefactor, Browne Willis.
>
> With Thanks from St Martins Parochial Church Council

Sandra Ritchie

On Friday, it was an amazing day for me to witness the Fenny Poppers being lit up in person for the first time in years. My mum Maureen, being a Fenny girl for many years, was chuffed when I decided to take her down to Leon Park to watch them going off for Remembrance Day.

As we saw some old familiar faces I was reminded how much my late nan (Glenys Healey) would have loved to see it all again, but she sadly passed away a few years ago. However, I was offered a privileged opportunity to light one of the poppers in memory of my nan. It was a true honour. Thank you to everyone involved for a special afternoon.

Gem Clare Grc

VE DAY

There were VE Day celebrations with street parties in cities, towns and villages right across the country. Bletchley was no exception.

Jean Blane Flannery

VE Day celebration - Saffron Street, Water Eaton
Photo posted by John Sheaf

The next photos, of an Oxford Street party, are from Terry Foster.

Getting the preparations under way
The young lad leaning on the railings doesn't look very impressed!

The party begins!

It's well underway now and there are some familiar faces here. Terry Foster is the little blond boy being carried on his mum's shoulders at the back.

Carole Cobb recognises Sarah Varney, holding her grandson Melvyn. They are in front of and to the left of Terry and the woman in the hat as you look at the photo. She also recognises her lovely mother-in-law Gertie Cobb, wearing a headscarf - toward the far right of the photo.

This image is thought to show members of the section known as Hut 6 celebrating VE Day. Notice the mix of men and women, military personnel and civilians that made up the section.

Thanks to Alan Andrews for this photo, which includes the caption.

Jean Flannery

CORONATION OF QUEEN ELIZABETH II 2 JUNE 1953

All the Bletchley Road Infant School children are seen holding up the coronation mugs they had just been presented with. These mugs were distributed to children all over the country.

Kathleen Roberts

Coronation mug that was given to all the children

Jean Blane Flannery

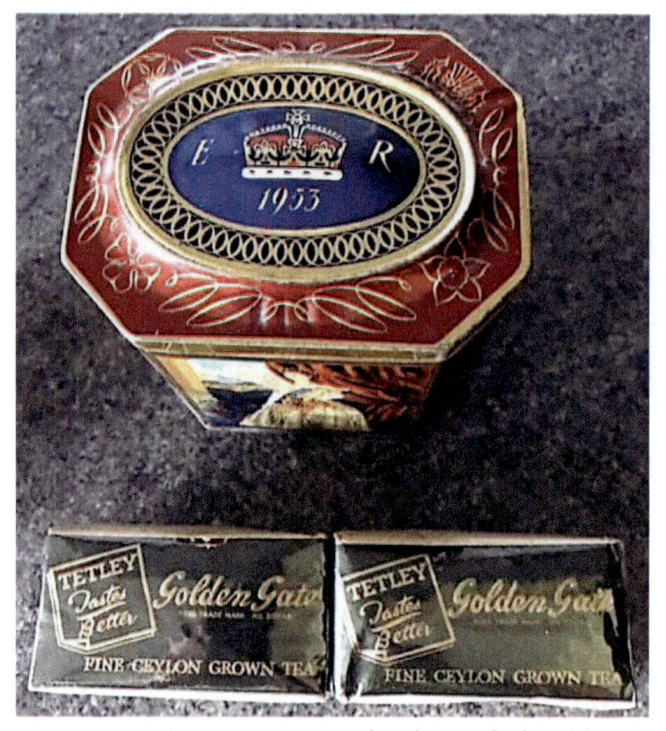

A coronation memory with a hint of Bletchley

Ann Elliott Stephens

We were living at 106 Western Road on Coronation Day.

There was a children's fancy dress contest. Mum made the costumes from crêpe paper for my cousin Ken Cutts, younger sister Carole, and me. I was "Red, White and Blue" (with a crown). Carole was "Hip, Hip, Hurray!'" and Ken was "Royal Herald."

I felt very miffed that Ken went on to actually win the competition in an outfit made by **my** mother.

The next picture was taken in our back garden, Dad's cabbages and the neighbours' washing as backdrop!

 We all shivered in our costumes, as the day was cold for June and it rained too. But it was still a truly special day. I remember being given a souvenir mug and plate.

Flags and bunting were to be seen everywhere around the town and there were a number of public celebrations. We went to a children's party in a local church hall, I think the Salvation Army Citadel in Church Street. A celebratory tea with sandwiches, jelly and cake, was laid on for us.

Jean Blane Flannery

Taken at the corner of Western Road, families hurrying off to a Coronation party. Photo courtesy of Living Archives

Friends and neighbours from Eaton Avenue celebrating in Bletchley Road School. Back row 3rd from left is Peggy Basketfield.

Diane McLean

I think Mrs Sear (Olive?) is the highest one on the back row. I wasn't born until 1962 but I wish I knew more of the people in the photo.

Mrs Sear lived at number 52. Her husband Fred was a brilliant gardener. I remember fondly going and knocking on the back door with a sixpence for a lettuce.

Their grandson Craig used to come and stay in the school holidays and we played cricket in the garden. Happy days!

Dianne Tofield

Sheila and Isabel Brown, their two older sisters and their mother are on the left of the photograph.

Donnah Lewis

The following photo of the Cub Scouts was found and shared by Judi Heavens.

BLETCHLEY AND FENNY TAPESTRY OF THOUGHTS

1 Elm Terrace, later to be 89 Church Green Road, decorated for the coronation.

Pamela Essam

Reg Pacey's coronation display

Valerie Young

Coronation Fun Cash in Expert Hands

MOST of the money Bletchley's street groups collect goes into the Trustee Savings Bank, and it is interesting to note that the manager of the bank and his wife are treasurer and secretary respectively of their own street group, while Mr. J. Litchfield, of Barclays Bank, is chairman of that same group.

The eighty or more children in the Bletchley-road, Albert-street, Park-street and South-terrace group will all have crown pieces set in boxes, as souvenirs of their celebrations.

The Albert-street Youth Centre has been booked for the day and the programme includes sports in the Albert-street field, tea and fancy dress. Grown-ups will have their "do" at a social the following Monday.

Group members pay what they can towards the day and so far £43 14s. 9d. has been banked.

When the first meeting was held the three bank officials were appointed—Mr. J. Litchfield as chairman, Mrs. V. M. Pearce as secretary, and Mr.

MRS. V. M. PEARCE
R. T. Pearce as treasurer. The committee includes Mrs. Walpole, Mrs. Gibbons, Mrs. Buckingham, Mr. Lane, Mr. T. Cloran and Mr. Herbert.

The sports committee is Mr. Hartwell, Mr. Lane, Mr. Gray and Mr. Beckett and tea committee; Mrs. Hartwell, Mrs. Mills, Mrs. Herbert and Mrs. Buckingham, who with others

MR. V. COOKE
will provide the "eats" on the day. Collectors are Mrs. Walpole, Mrs. Dewhurst, Mrs. Gibbons, Mrs. Herbert, Mrs. Buckingham and Mrs. Lane.

The youngest street group

Youngest street group is Victoria-road, officially inaugurated a week ago, though arrangements started three weeks earlier.

Actually it has been set up because of the offer of adjoining George-street who invited some of the nearby Victoria-road tenants to join in their fun.

Mrs. W. Wallis, Mr. J. Parriss and Mr. and Mrs. V. Cooke called a meeting of all Victoria-road people and decided they should do something for the whole street.

Mr. H. Allen arranged for the use of the Bletchley-road Methodist hut for Thursday's meeting when Mr. Parriss was elected chairman, Mr. V. Cooke secretary and treasurer, and Mrs. Wallis and Mrs. Cooke official collectors.

The entertainments committee is Mr. M. A. Thomas, Miss

Hames and Mr. Wright, and the catering committee Mr. Dice, Mrs. Wallis, Mrs. Cooke and Mrs. Walpole.

There are some 70 members with 30 children and 30 old age pensioners and altogether it is planned that 140 people will be catered for on the day.

Arrangements are still in an early stage but already competitions have been arranged to raise money. The Bletchley-road Methodist hut has been hired for the day and Messrs. M. A. Cook and Son have offered their forecourt for celebrations.

There will be a tea for all and it is hoped, a fancy dress parade for children and adults. Some sort of souvenir will also be bought for presentation to the children.

Brooklands-road group

Brooklands-road Coronation group which now has 66 members started in a very small way early in December when several

the old age pensioners in the "children's tea," and even all contributors if funds will allow. There will be sweets, ices, souvenirs and a fancy dress parade for the children.

The group officers are: Mr. Day, chairman; Mrs. R. North, Secretary; and Mrs. Matthews and Mrs. Graham (who live next door to each other) joint treasurer-collectors.

The committee is Mr. S. Felce, Mrs. Howe, Mrs. Bond, Mrs. S. Felce, Mrs. Thomas, Mrs. Slater, Mrs. Knowles and Mrs. Sanders.

Mrs. J. F. Ramsbotham has offered a room at her house for meetings, Mr. Ramsbotham a large packing shed should the day be wet, Mrs. B. R. Reynolds has offered her garden for the day.

Collections are made monthly and these have been augmented by a competition. So far the total is £26.

MRS. R. NORTH
parents approached Mr. S. Felce and suggested a street party.

Mr. Felce approached Mrs. R. North, of 48 Brooklands-road, who has three children and on December 8 the first meeting was held at Mr. Felce's house.

The plan now is to include

Newspaper cutting courtesy of Clive Gough

GUY FAWKES DAY

Remember, remember the 5th of November
Gunpowder, treason and plot
I see no reason why gunpowder treason
Should ever be forgot

Guy Fawkes didn't know what he started! This topic arguably "sparked" more interest in our members than almost any other. I have tried to make the chapter a representative selection of all the great stories shared.

Jean Blane Flannery

Bletchley Gazette 1963, Larch Grove - thanks to Eddie Mac

Left to right: Eddie Mac, Richard McErlane, Billy Robinson, Trevor Tom Linton, Roger Jacobs, Paul Kearns, Gareth Doyle, Colin Walker

This brings back many memories of bonfire night in Newton Road. The neighbourhood kids spent ages building a big bonfire in the rec, only for someone to set fire to it before the 5th

Liz Jackson

Being a Larch Grove lad myself, 1963 was a bit late for me as I was already at work. There was always competition between us and Chestnut Crescent though, with occasional spontaneous ignitions before the day!!

Mike Blane

I remember when we used to build bonfires. We competed with Pinewood Drive across the brook. Larch Grove was always the best.

Kay McErlane

I remember collecting for the big bonfire at the bottom of Chestnut Crescent. All of us children took turns keeping watch in case Larch Grove children tried to set fire to it.

Pat Bateman

Bring back competition! I can remember Tony Redhead being dressed as the guy and wheeling him in a barrow down to the Plough pub: "Penny for the guy!" We never did manage to sell him!

Linda Slater

Francis Emmerton and I used make a guy and sit under the railway bridge, waiting for commuters coming home on the trains.

Marie Love

Strange to tell, I did exactly that too!

Terry Foster

We used to push a guy we made out of newspaper, straw and old clothes around Eaton Avenue in my dad's wheelbarrow. We then sat the guy on a chair indoors until bonfire night, because my sister and I thought it looked funny. Dad built a big bonfire in the allotment at the bottom of our garden.

On bonfire night Dad lit the bonfire with the guy on the top. We felt a little sad that our creation was being burned now, but also excited. Dad set off fireworks in the garden and we waved sparklers. We had hotdogs and milkshakes. Great memories as a child growing up in Bletchley.

Christine Barlow

I remember we used to start going round collecting rubbish for our fire in early October, storing the stuff in our various sheds until a week before. Then we built our fire on the rec between St John's Road and Newton Road. All the kids would gather over there with their sparklers on bonfire night.

Mum always made us Lancashire hotpot in the evening, before going over to the fire. She would also make toffee apples to take over.

We had some real big fires there in my time. We took it in turns to guard against rival estate bonfire builders coming to steal our wood, or worse set it alight. There was fierce competition as to who could build best. There was a rival gang that built a fire at the top of St Clement's, near Whaddon way. They were forever trying to sabotage ours, and probably vice versa: we were no angels.

Eileen Neath

We always had a bonfire that my dad was in charge of, although right up to the night he would say we couldn't have one!

He would bring home a couple of telegraph pole arms. Those were tarred so the blaze was amazing, no matter what other rubbish had been stored away in the dustbin cupboard to keep it dry.

We fetched out our shoe box containing the fireworks, to add to the box that dad had bought on his way home from work. Large potatoes were put into the hot embers and after all the excitement Dad would take them out. They were delicious! Today's jacket spuds have nothing on them.

It was always a fun time for children, which leaves us with wonderful memories.

Kathleen Roberts

We always had fireworks. Dad was in charge, Catherine wheels hammered on to the fence loosely with a nail. I used to watch them spinning around. Rocket standing in a glass milk bottle: light the touch paper and stand back waiting for the rocket to rise up into the sky. And the sparklers, making words with them in the air. The jacket potatoes and hot soup to warm you up. Oh the memories, happy days.

Sheila Batham

We had a village bonfire in Bow Brickhill. Everyone collected for the bonfire and we all got clothes to make a guy. The bonfire was in one of farmer Carter's fields, the fireworks controlled by the adults. We had jacket potatoes cooked in the fire. Great days, lovely memories

Prudence Williams

Every bonfire night my mum made parkin (much like gingerbread), along with bonfire toffee made with black treacle. That stuck to our teeth seemingly forever but it was good!

As well as the other fireworks, I remember penny bangers and jumping jacks. Lit and thrown to the ground, we used to hop around quite a bit when a jumping jack was nearby.

Jean Blane Flannery

Shenley Brook End's village green, at the junction of the Whaddon,

Bletchley and Church End roads, was the site for the huge Guy Fawkes night bonfire. We village children took our old go-carts and prams around the 40 houses, collecting anything and everything that would go up in flames!

Bonfire night saw a big gathering on the green of locals and those from other localities for some years, lots of fireworks and potatoes roasted in the embers, until it was discontinued.

But one year stands out to me for the wrong reason. We had made a "cave" inside our massive bonfire. One afternoon, the heavens opened and it began thundering and lightning.

I threw down my new red bike and we dived into the cave for cover, even though my house was only 50 metres away.

It was dark and my parents were worried. Dad came looking for me, saw my bike and hauled me home. I had a lovely hot bath - followed by my only heavy spanking from dad, afterwards being sent to bed with no food. I have never forgotten that year!

Judith Kutty

If the next day was a school day, on the way there the boys would collect the spent fireworks. To this day I don't know why. They then had to throw them in a bin near the school. I suppose it cleared up the pathways.

Kathleen Roberts

Waking up the morning after bonfire night was always special to us as kids. The smell of gunpowder/smoke still lingered in the air. The dying embers of the bonfire had a definite magic.

We couldn't wait to throw on our clothes, knock for each other and go collecting the empty firework shells, stirring up the bonfire ash to see if any sparks remained.

One year in the early sixties my best friend and next door neighbour Liz Jackson and I woke up to big trouble. It would seem we suddenly had an open plan garden? The fence seemed to have disappeared!

Well, if anyone can remember the council house fences in Newton Road you will appreciate what excellent "pokers" those wooden stakes made!! They kept the bonfire going for hours.

As I say, we woke up to big trouble and we've never been allowed to forget it. Kids, eh ? The things you do.

There's even a post missing from the fence in this picture! Whiteley Crescent and Mr Claridge's greenhouse are behind us.

Diane McLean

REMEMBRANCE

Year unknown, the Boys' Brigade on parade on Remembrance Sunday.

Pam Essam

11 November 1946, Guides with Joyce Basketfield on parade at the war memorial.

Diane McLean

MALCOLM WHEELER

Our own Malcolm Wheeler works tirelessly with Bletchley Freemasons for the Poppy Day Appeal, which he organises: a very big job.

He and a team of fellow Freemasons also keep the borders around the Bletchley and Fenny Stratford War Memorial planted up and looking beautiful.

Malcolm gives his all in everything he does for the community, going above and beyond any call of duty.

Jean Blane Flannery

Here is a small selection of Malcolm's Remembrance and Poppy Day posts over the past few years.

2018 Bletchley and Fenny Stratford Town Council organised a Remembrance Day Parade. Local Freemasons were proud to take part. After the parade, the Bletchley Masonic Centre opened its doors for refreshments, and was attended by over 100 people.

2020 Bletchley Freemasons planted some 400 bedding plants in the borders of the Bletchley and Fenny Stratford War Memorial today.

Many thanks to Libby & Jim Marsh of Fabric World for their most generous donation of all the plants.

2023 Freemasons from the Bletchley Masonic Centre planted the Queensway Memorial with summer bedding over the Bank Holiday Weekend.

Bletchley Poppy Appeal 2023

Poppy Appeal Wreath Range

A Wreath
Spray of poppies approx. 7" diameter (plus stem and leaves)
Price £15

B Wreath
17" diameter wreath of all poppies with an open center
Price £20

C Wreath
17" diameter wreath of all poppies with badge of choice, if required
Price £25 without a badge or £27.50 with a badge

F Wreath
17" diameter wreath of all poppies
Price £25

We are currently taking orders for your Remembrance Wreaths. To order please contact The Bletchley Poppy Appeal Organiser.

Bletchley Poppy Appeal 2023
Freemasonry in the Community

We are looking for volunteers to assist in the years poppy appeal.

1. *To help make up the poppy boxes Monday 16th October. (At Bletchley Masonic Centre)*
2. *Delivering poppy boxes from Wednesday 18th October (In and around Bletchley)*
3. *Collecting poppy boxes and £ tins Monday 13th November*
4. *Counting money at Bletchley Masonic Centre from Wednesday 15th November.*
5. *Manning the Poppy Stand at Bletchley Tesco from Thursday 26th October to Saturday 11th November. (Full or Half days)*

If you can help, please contact The Bletchley Poppy Appeal Organiser W. Bro Malcolm Wheeler

Over 28,000 poppies boxed up today by Freemasons working in and for the community.

BIG thanks to Allan Casey (Brickhill Lodge), Ewan Gordon (Emergency Services), and Peter Loake (Loungville Lodge) for volunteering to help today.

Now we need a few volunteers to deliver them.

The 2023 Bletchley Poppy Appeal Raised £56,364.10

A **BIG** thank you to all who helped in raising this fantastic amount

I'm pleased to say we raised a record amount this year despite the shortage of volunteers.

Malcolm Wheeler

My dad Jim Cusack, just after receiving his gold bar and certificates from the British Legion for 50yrs of Poppy selling. Dad served in Burma through the 2nd World War.

We always went along to the service at the Bletchley Rd cenotaph. My dad led the parade for years. It used to be so long with all the different organisations of the town laying a wreath. The Boys' Brigade band would play and everyone on parade marched in time.

Once they got their left foot in time, Dad would call out, "By the left, quick march!" It was all timed out, right through the ranks, then it was, "Parade, halt!" Afterwards, the parade went up to St Mary's cenotaph and a service was held.

In the afternoon they went over to Simpson and had a church service there too. I would imagine it would still be very much the same, if the groups participated.

Kathleen Roberts

2018

Arwel Rees-Kay, trumpeter for Last Post and Reveille

Well done to the organisers of today's Remembrance Commemorations in Fenny Stratford/Bletchley. It was good turnout, fitting the occasion.

Douglas Sellers

2023

I have been up to St Mary's Church, to leave my poppy in remembrance of my dad's half-brother Reuben Howard Hanton (Will), who was killed in 1918.

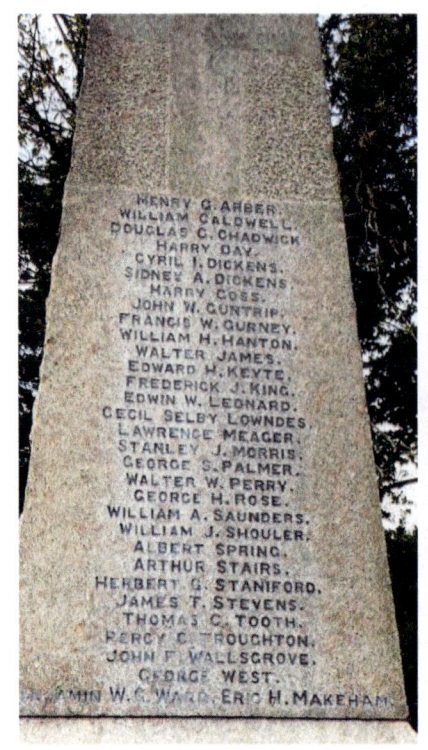

Pamela Essam

CHRISTMAS PAST

This first story was written in 2007 by my Uncle Don, who was born 19 October 1908. In 1917 he had two older brothers, two younger, and a younger sister. My father was born in 1918, followed two years later by Martin, the youngest sibling.

Jean Blane Flannery

As I celebrate my 99th Christmas, I look back to the Christmases I remember as a boy 90 years ago. There was no electricity, radio, TV, telephone or refrigeration. A motor vehicle was seldom seen - transportation was by horse and cart or railway.

Preparations for Christmas started in November, when Mother made several puddings and a cake. The pudding mixture included a number of silver coins called threepenny bits. The boys were allowed to stir the mixture "for luck." The puddings were boiled for 5 or 6 hours in a coal-fired copper boiler.

My mother provided a roll of coloured wallpaper for the boys to cut into strips and make paper-chains, which were hung at ceiling level from corner to corner. We had to be careful to avoid the heat from the gaslight, which was on a pendant in the centre.

In the evenings Henry and I would go out and sing carols to get some pennies for Christmas. A candle in a jamjar was used to light the way. The only street lights were gas, which had to be lit and extinguished every night and morning by a lamplighter.

There was great excitement on Christmas Eve when each boy called "up the chimney" to ask Father Christmas for the gift he would like. Stockings would be hung up in a row for filling. The boys would all be up early to find out what Santa had left.

In each stocking there might be - an orange, a white sugar mouse, a packet of sweet cigarettes, a ball or a top to spin. The main presents would be on the table with labels.

Depending on age there might be: coloured building blocks, a set of lead soldiers, Lego, a Meccano set, a tin of paints with a brush, a Hobby's fretwork set, a soccer ball or boots. The children would play with their toys up to dinner-time at 12.30pm.

We never had turkey. We kept hens and one or two cockerels in a garden pen. The cockerels would be cooped up a few weeks before Christmas for fattening.

It was a splendid meal, with Christmas pudding and custard, everyone hoping to find a silver coin and careful not to swallow before checking.

The Christmas cake would be eaten at tea-time (4.30pm) followed by each one pulling a cracker to find a paper hat and motto.

In the front room, or parlour, a coal fire would have been lit in the morning. There was a small Christmas tree decorated with tinsel and ornaments (no electric lights). After tea, we would all go into the front room.

Mother had a small harp, which she played while she sang. The boys played with their toys and roasted chestnuts in the hot ashes under the grate. Then we all played card games like Fish and Rummy until it was bedtime.

"And Santa, laying his finger aside of his nose, called out 'Merry Christmas!' as up the chimney he rose."

Donald Blane

In 1971-73 I worked for the Royal Mail delivering Christmas Post. Official secrets act signed, I was a loyal employee crossing through unfranked stamps so that they couldn't be reused. I have many happy memories of frosty, breezy, icy mornings wrapped up in my yellow bell bottoms, duffle coat and woolly scarf heading for the pick-up point - the Shoulder of Mutton.

The coach took us to the sorting office where it was all hands on deck - huge bags of mail waiting to be franked, sorted and delivered. We were kept busy before our deliveries and the air of festive excitement was tangible. There was a real sense of fun and camaraderie amongst the staff. After a hot cuppa we were on our way.

My route was a bit rural, fair bit of leg work with some long gated drives - not all welcoming - and running the gauntlet of the odd ferocious beast was not great. I have always maintained that the jobs you do in life are character building.

The funniest thing was delivering a whole fresh salmon - imagine getting that through your letter box. I really couldn't contain my laughter and I have actually dined out on that story so many times.

Since then though I have even sent kippers and clotted cream through the post myself to family and friends over the years, wondering if the cat got there first.

Me 30 years later, having just posted some kippers to Mum from Malaig. I am still laughing my head off as I remember trying to fit that salmon through the letterbox of some poor unsuspecting guy.

And before you ask, Dad did get to the door before the cat!

Diane McLean

I did three or four stints like that in Bletchley in 1964-67. For two or three of them I was delivering door-to-door in the estates in the north-west, but one year I had a cushy number.

That was transferring sacks of mail that had arrived by train to the sorting office behind the GPO in Bletchley Road. So I sat in the cab of a warm PO van or in the Coffee Knob, drinking cups of hot tea between trains.

Nick Halewood

I remember my nan making Christmas puddings in a great big bowl that was used years ago, with a jug, as a basin for washing yourself before they had bathrooms. She used to put in grated carrot and apple, and always sixpence wrapped in a little tin foil. Then the bottle of stout went in and we all had a stir.

I make my own Christmas cake, used to make my own puddings too but gave that up a few years ago. My family all love Christmas cake and puddings.

Sandra Ritchie

The first intimation of Christmas every year came towards the end of November, when Mum made the Christmas puddings. As she mixed them we all had to have a stir and make a wish. Then the kitchen was filled with steam as they cooked for hours. In my early years they were steamed in the washing boiler.

Some were given away to relatives and the rest kept. The pudding eaten on Christmas Day was always one made the year before. It would seem that like a good wine they matured with keeping.

I didn't much care for Christmas Pudding but always had a small piece. Mum put old, real silver, thruppenny bits in the pudding mix.

If you found one in your piece of pudding, Mum swapped it for a modern sixpence.

As younger children my cousin Ken Cutts and I made Christmas presents of calendars. We stuck a picture cut from a birthday card or out of a magazine on to a piece of stiff card. Then we attached a little calendar, bought from the stationer's (Smith's I suppose), to the bottom of this with ribbon or tape. Sometimes we glued glitter onto the pictures. We were very proud of these calendars.

Presents weren't placed round the tree or seen at all before Christmas Day. On Christmas morning I woke to a stocking and pillowcase full of presents at the foot of my bed. The stocking with its small presents smelled of tangerine and of a lemon shaped, strongly lemon scented soap - lovely! I emptied the stocking there and then but my sister and I opened all the bigger presents together on Mum and Dad's bed.

Jean Blane Flannery

We had farming friends and every Christmas they visited us, bringing with them a capon for Mum to cook on Christmas Day. They also gifted us walnuts picked from the tree in their garden and a bag of straw used for hibernating my pal Tommy Tortoise.

We had my dear mum's home-made mince pies and other such delights, with lots of merriment. Sugar mice, oh yes, complete with their string tails! My dad always bought my mum Payne's Brazil nuts in milk chocolate and a box of Milk Tray.

Dorothy (the farmer's daughter, now in her mid 80s) and I still share memories of Christmas past. A time of innocence when life wasn't so challenging, or at least that's how it seemed.

Ann Elliott Stephens

Every year my lovely granny filled a truly magical stocking for me. It was white netting edged with a red crêpe paper trim. You could see all of the treasures inside and some even broke through, adding to the magic of the moment. I have spent the last three decades of my life searching for one. One year I made two coasters for my nan and grampy. Nan kept them and treasured them for over 60 years, bless her.

I inevitably seemed to get a Knitting Nancy, as it seems did many others.

Diane McLean

One year we had a poor little scraggly tree that was overlooked until my dad, who was late getting ours, was offered it for 6 bob! He bought it and it was planted out in the back garden after Christmas. Although never brought inside again, Mum would decorate it with food for the birds all year round. It grew for over 30 years into the most magnificent tree, until the present owner of the house had to chop it down

Kathleen Roberts

We never had turkey and despite being so rural I have never eaten it! Dad selected a certain number of young cockerels early on in the year to be kept separate from the main poultry. One by one he killed them and removed most of the feathers before bringing them in. We then singed the remaining pieces of feather with paraffin and newspaper. It was mostly Mum and I who did all the "cleaning" of the birds, which were given or sold to relatives and others.

The one we had for Christmas was stuffed with fresh thyme, sage, onions from our garden and breadcrumbs. With a struggle the massive cockerel, its legs tied together with string, covered in various greases and grease proof paper, began his several hours roasting in the wood fired Rayburn and came out looking decidedly tanned and crisp.

Only Dad carved any meat that graced the dining table - with a lethal old bread knife that he sharpened on a pumice stone. If a child touched it he said, "It'll cut your head off!" Tender and juicy meat, freshly picked Brussel sprouts (picked covered in ice, your fingers feeling as if they were dropping off until hot ache set in), roast spuds etc, followed by the six month matured Christmas pudding and custard.

Judith Kutty

I remember that as a child we always went to church at 10am. That meant we had to wait to play with our new toys etc until returning home, where we were met by the lovely aroma of the dinner roasting, Christmas type puddings and fruits adding to the wonderful scent as we entered the house.

My dad used to buy my mum a really big tin of Quality Street and one of those lovely boxes of chocolates with the pretty thatched cottage on the front that you don't see today. We senior school girls used the tins to take all our cookery ingredients in for our cookery lessons: oh what memories eh!

Kathleen Roberts

Our fairy has been on our Christmas trees every year since 1965. I bought her in Woolworths, Bletchley!

Carole Purcell

In between the stories of enjoyment and merriment, we find reminders of less happy Christmases. Here are two...

My mother was a great cook and she produced lovely Christmas dinners. The only one that really stands out though was in 1973, shortly after my father had died. I went home from Clacton, where I was teaching, and Christmas dinner was a cheese sandwich made by me. My mother wouldn't even have her usual gin and lime. A very sad time.

Alan Jones

In 1940, after Dunkirk and marrying Mum in the October, Dad had his last Christmas in England until 1944. His words:

"Our unit left Liverpool in December 1941 and we spent Christmas Day that year in Sierra Leone harbour.

I spent Christmas 1942 at Tobruk and New Year's Eve at Benghazi. Then it was on to the last battle for the 8th Army in North Africa.

After that we went to Malta for two weeks' rest and then it was the invasion of Sicily and into Southern Italy. Our ship came under heavy fire while we lay off Italy prior to landing.

We sailed for England from Bari on a lousy, overcrammed ship. We had half a ration of bully beef for Christmas dinner 1943. At night all the floors, the dining tables and hammocks, were full of men."

Forever after, Dad loved and treasured his family Christmases.

Jean Blane Flannery

Ending on a happier note, though it was rather hard on Rosemary...

We had to give one of our presents to the church on Christmas morning for children less fortunate than us. it was a hard decision as to what to take!

I remember looking outside for our aunts and uncles arriving to have Christmas dinner with us. And in the 1950s it was like heaven for us all to share a tin of Quality Street, not like today.

Rosemary Sellars

We were three "Gazzers" that have Christmas Day birthdays. The Bletchley Gazette did a small feature on us, I would guess about 1978.

The boy at the bottom is Mark Carey. I am the one in the middle but I'm afraid I have no idea who the top girl is.

Teresa Sinclair

LET'S GO SHOPPING

SO MANY SHOPS

Bletchley and Fenny combined formed a bustling small market town, with all the shops you could need whether you were on a mission or just window shopping.

Let's start as we enter Bletchley from Station Approach. First we have the "tin shops" on the left, and opposite those next to the Park Hotel, the Co-op butchery managed by my Uncle Reg Cutts.

Past the tin shops and the entrance to the station yard, a real variety awaits us. We'll make our way along Bletchley Road, all the way to the small parade of shops with Gilroy's Fashions being one, as we approach Fenny's Victoria Road.

BLETCHLEY AND FENNY TAPESTRY OF THOUGHTS

Past the tin shops and Station Yard we go, now looking back.

Above: the old Co-op and beyond. Next we head further into town.

We carry on, now on the other side of the road

And then we look towards the Studio and beyond

Beyond the Studio we find what was then the New Inn, small parade of shops beyond and Bletchley Road School back right.

At the rear of the picture, out of shot, is the left turn to Victoria Road, Fenny.

Looking back past the little parade of shops that included Gilroy's, towards the New Inn and the Studio with its bright white side.

Now we'll leave Bletchley and move briefly into the main Fenny shopping streets.

Victoria Road is first, looking down towards Bletchley Road.

Then Aylesbury Street, looking along from St Martin's Church.

That concludes our brief trip around the main shopping areas of Bletchley and Fenny. And now we move on to individual shops, starting with the well-remembered Co-op department store.

THE CO-OP

The Co-op department store: a Bletchley landmark and icon. This is the building most of us will remember, rebuilt in the 1950s after a fire. The original building at the far end was demolished.

The Co-op was the largest shop in Bletchley. It was huge in comparison to the other shops, and a wonderland to many local children.

The payment system in the Co-op was fascinating. The shop assistant wrote a bill and took your money. Then the money and bill were placed in a lidded tub. The assistant pushed this tub up into a clear plastic vertical tube, which it just fitted.

As the tub went into the tube, it shot up and then along under the ceiling to disappear we knew not where. Soon after, back came the tub with a receipt and any change.

There was a grid of horizontal tubes under the ceiling and a vertical tube from each counter intersecting this grid, so you could often see several tubs at a time whizzing about to and fro. I could quite happily watch that while Mum shopped.

I know now that it was some kind of pneumatic system but when I was small it seemed almost like magic.

Jean Blane Flannery

I used to love the air tubes taking your money to the office and your change and receipt coming back.

Alan Andrews

Whoosh !   Clunk!

Mum would work in every fabric then available from finest silk to taffeta to velvet. I can still hear her sewing machine and when Mum was laying out the Simplicity Paper patterns I would pin them down for her. That said, she had this special genius. She could see someone wearing a dress and then reproduce it without using a pattern.

Given the cost of fabrics in the early 1950s, when buying fabrics at the Co-op or from Mrs Tookey's stall on Thursdays at Bletchley Market, she always knew - to the inch - how much was needed. Let me just say that Mum's sewing machine and Dadda's brickie trowel put me through university.

John Goss

This photo of the 1934 Co-op Management Committee is also thanks to John Goss.

BLETCHLEY AND FENNY TAPESTRY OF THOUGHTS

Two cards that missed the Christmas Post.

For many years Co-op staff received a card designed by the very talented local artist Kathleen Thompson née Fryer.

Kathleen grew up in Eaton Avenue, the daughter of the late Alderman Ernest J Fryer who was a Director of the Co-operative Society and its President for 20 years until his retirement in 1975.

Diane McLean

My Uncle Bob Blane was secretary of the Bakery Department (the department winning national awards), before becoming manager. Then he was on the Co-op Advisory Board and later the Committee, of which he was also secretary.

Co-op Board members 1966, Bob Blane far right

My Uncle Martin Blane was a Co-op insurance agent. He might have come knocking at your door to collect the premiums, who knows?

So let's not forget the Co-op grocery, dairy, butchery, bakery, laundry, insurance arm... The Co-op touched just about every aspect of our lives - and deaths, with the Co-op funeral service. It was integral to Bletchley and to my family as to many others.

The Co-op butcher's shop was next to the Park Hotel, deliveries made by boys on bicycles. My Uncle Reg Cutts managed the butchery for over 30 years, until his death in 1963.

You couldn't hang meat and poultry as seen in the following picture from the 1930s nowadays! But back then it was the way the butcher's shop front was dressed every Christmas season.In the photo, left to right, are John Rowe, my Uncle Reg, Archie White,

Len Walduck, Dick Goodman and Ben Smith. I'm afraid the final person on the right is a mystery.

The Co-op had a number of smaller grocery shops and if you wished, you could have your groceries delivered. You wrote your order in a special carboned book and took it into the shop. When the groceries were delivered you had one copy of the order as an invoice and then paid for the groceries.

You could have milk and bread delivered, buying plastic milk and bread checks (tokens). Leave the number of milk checks on the front doorstep for the number of pint bottles you wanted that day and they would be delivered.

Order your bread for delivery. If you were going out, hang a bag on the front door knob or handle, or leave it by the door, with the bread check in it, and your loaf would be there.

The "butcher's boy" too delivered on his bicycle.

Jean Blane Flannery

I did a Saturday Co-op bread round with old Jock. He would give me a bag of left over cakes for my mum! I also remember the various tokens people would leave outside, representing the type of loaf that they had paid for at the shop.

William McLaughlin

For those who used the service, dirty laundry was collected from your house when booked. It was washed, dried, pressed and delivered folded back to your door.

Of course, all these transactions earned you Co-op "divi" (dividend) just as shop purchases did. Oh, that Co-op divi!

Every member of the Co-operative Society was a shareholder. They had a dividend number and whenever they bought anything from any department, they received a receipt that was like a little ticket.

The total spent and the dividend number were hand-written on this. These tickets were in sheets, again in a carboned book so the Co-op had a copy too.

As the customers of the Co-op were its shareholders, each year the net profit was divided up between them. They received dividend money proportional to how much they had spent over the previous year as a whole.

This 'divi' came in very handy, especially coming up to Christmas time. Many of us still remember our mum's, or even our own, divi numbers!

Jean Blane Flannery

MR WILLIAM GOLDING'S SHOP

Let's hear it for the legendary Mr Golding with his iconic delivery vehicle, a man who will be remembered for his delicious ice-cream for which people would walk miles.

Diane McLean

Oh my, the best ice cream ever; it was delicious. Every weekend I used to go to his shop and get an ice cream cornet, some Blue Bird toffees, and Merry Maid toffees covered in chocolate for my mum.

The story has it he took the ice cream recipe to the grave with him.

Sheila Batham

Sometimes Mum gave me money to buy an ice cream after Sunday School at the Spurgeon Memorial Baptist Church - very handy!

We'd often take a bowl to be filled with that delicious ice cream when we were round at Cambridge Street for tea in the summer. I think my Uncle Reg Cutts usually drove us there, making sure the ice cream didn't melt before we got it back. Happy days!

Jean Blane Flannery

Every Sunday my sister Shirley and I had one after Sunday School.

I'm not sure where the money came from because I can remember Shirley saying we had to finish them before we got home!!

Norma Chambers

Just the best ever ice cream. Mr Golding won many prizes for it and had the certificates hanging in the shop.

Unfortunately the ice lollies were not so good. Oh umm!

Kathleen Roberts

Here's that iconic delivery cart, ready to be restocked.

HARRINGTON'S HANDCRAFTS

> **THE ONLY REAL HOBBY SHOP IN THE DISTRICT**
>
> **ARTS & CRAFTS** MATERIALS, TOOLS, Etc. FELTS, LEATHERS, RAFFIA, SEAGRASS, STOOL FRAMES, LAMPSHADE FRAMES & COVERINGS, FIRESCREEN FRAMES
>
> **HOBBIES** Machines Outfits and Designs
>
> **HARRINGTON'S HANDCRAFTS**
> 3 VICTORIA RD., BLETCHLEY
>
> Meccano
> Dinky Toys
> Hornby Trains
> Juneero Kits
>
> **MODEL AEROS, SHIPS AND CARS**
> KITS, PLANS, AND ACCESSORIES in STOCK
>
> **MODEL RAILWAYS**
> AUTHORISED STOCKISTS for HAMBLINGS, PECO, STEWART REIDPATH, MILBRO & OTHER LEADING MAKES
>
> TOYS . GAMES . NOVELTIES . DOLLS' HOSPITAL

Thanks to Diane McLean for this advertisement

Harrington's craft shop in Victoria Road was wonderful. The windows were filled with every kind of toy, craft and hobby item imaginable. If you wanted it, Harrington's had it!

Mr Harrington also repaired dolls in his "Dolls' Hospital," fondly remembered by many.

The old fashioned shop bell told Mr and Mrs Harrington when they had customers. Mr Harrington came out of his back workshop when he heard its ring.

He specialised in Keil Kraft model aeroplanes, often having some assembled and hanging from the shop ceiling.

Another speciality was doll house furniture. The quality of the items was so good that collectors sought them out, travelling from quite some distance to buy them.

Many locals have happy memories either of purchases or, as children with no money, gazing longingly at all the toys in the window.

It was a sad day when Mr and Mrs Harrington retired and closed the shop. Bletchley now has nothing like it.

Jean Blane Flannery

I had a Saturday job there in the 1960s and remember both Mr and Mrs Harrington. Unfortunately my practical skills were nil, so I think I lasted less than a year.

Mr Harrington was a good guy but his circular saw in the shed at the end of the garden caused me real stress when he asked me to use it.

Glenn Warren

I used to shop in there as I made paper flowers and they had loads of materials to choose from.

Linda Shadbolt

My doll spent time in there and I still have her to this day

Prudence Williams

One of my dolls was healed in the doll's hospital after her arm had mysteriously amputated itself!

Angela Evans

My doll was given a new head (melted from being left too close to the coal fire) but sadly nothing like the original.

I guess some transplants are more successful than others .

Diane McLean

JACK PARRISS' SHOP

Remembering Jack Parriss, a local tradesman who ran a tobacconist and confectionery shop at 11, Victoria Road.

Jack caught on camera in a very familiar pose

The queue outside his shop was characteristic of the day sweet rationing ended.

Kathleen Catalanotto, seen here, was in that queue with her bicycle on the day - treats all round.

Diane McLean

I remember him very well, he was a very good friend of my great uncle, Sid Marks. They played bowls together at St Martin's club and Jack came on holiday with my uncle and myself twice, once to Hastings and once to the Isle of Wight.

John Bowler

When we moved to Western Road, Mum would sometimes give me a penny to spend in Parriss' shop. I walked to school along Victoria Road and spent my penny on the way.

Walking into the shop, the smell alone transported me. Then the delight of seeing all those sweets that were 4 for a penny. But oh, the agony of making a decision.

On the odd occasion that I had a few extra pence I might buy sweet tobacco (shredded coconut tossed in sweetened cocoa powder), sweet cigarettes, a liquorice pipe, or a sherbet fountain. They cost so little and gave so much joy!

Here's a small selection of the sweets you could buy 4 for a penny.
Jean Blane Flannery

My nan and pop lived over the road (4 Victoria Road) from Parriss' sweet shop and we were very lucky to always get pocket money to spend in the shop. We used to get 4 for a penny sweets and I remember asking for "Withs and Withouts," Marshmallows either with or without being coated in toasted coconut.

Happy Days! Ann King

NEAL'S

A shop that I grew up with - a shop that is a household name to many, Neal's was The Shop for toys, games and models.

Edward Neal's parents had a retail shop in Croydon before moving to Bedfordshire.

Edward purchased "The Bletchley Bazaar" 1 December 1945, renaming it "The Bazaar." Opened for business in 1946 and first run by his parents, it soon became known simply as Neal's. It was a real family business, with a family member always on hand to help.

The Neal's claim to fame was that they were pioneers in the field of modernisation of their premises. For example, they were the first to install fluorescent lighting and the first to give a specialist toy and pram service to the town.

They were notable for their forward thinking in stocking their range of prams and nursery furniture in the years of rapid growth of the local population.

Many local babies will have been pushed around town in a pram or pushchair purchased from Neal's. I am seen here in my granny's garden in Eaton Avenue - 1953.

Diane McLean

I got my first baby's pram from Neals and paid weekly for it before the baby was born. It cost £28.10 shillings.

Pat Bateman

I can remember standing for ages using the rotating car display thing.

Grape Vine

Many of us have fond memories of a shop that once you entered seemed to go on and on and on - adding to the magic for us as kids That and Woolworth's were real treasure troves.

Diane McLean

It did seem to go on forever inside, so many different wonders to discover as you looked all around. I had no Woolworth's to compare it with at the time but I don't think Woolworth's could ever really have held a candle to Neal's for me!

Jean Blane Flannery

There I am in front of Mr Neal Snr, happy days. That's how I met Malcolm. He worked in Pollard's, and me in Neal's.

Malcolm walked by every day and the rest is history - 57 years married this May.

Jane Wheeler

I recognise Mr Neal and Edward. I used to play with the youngest, Philip. We often dressed up as Cowboys and Indians and had a teepee in the back garden. We had guns too.

Anne Falcus

Neal's celebrated 21 years of trading in 1967 and the family were rightly very proud of both their Bletchley and Leighton Buzzard stores.

It was a sad day for the town when they made the decision to close their doors and cease trading

Diane McLean

RAMSBOTHAMS FLORIST

Another family name vanishes from Bletchley Road (Queensway)

Malcolm Wheeler

Malcolm's recent post on the closure of Ramsbothams Florists was a very sad jolt for many. With the nurseries in Brooklands road sold up and filled with houses quite some time ago, it seems to me that Bletchley citizens have lost yet another piece of family and business history.

I'd just like to rewind some happy memories after spending my initial years after school and during college at Ramsbothams Nurseries in Brooklands road from the mid to late 1960s.

In those days it was common to see the elderly James Ramsbotham, (founder) pottering around the nursery. Although losing his eye sight he still had a good knowledge of who was who and what was what! His son Michael was hands on and running the business, daughter-in-law Gill in the office.

Stephanotis and ferns filled one humid greenhouse, plucked for the florist shop's bridal bouquets. Bedding plants went to Oxford and Buckingham markets, to be sold in the Bletchley Road shop, or planted out on contract in displays at the Central Gardens. Flowering plants were for shop sale or to decorate the stage at Wilton Hall.

From the large greenhouses over 30,000 lettuces were cut and packed for the summer salad market, together with hundreds of boxes of freshly picked tomatoes. Beautiful cut chrysanthemums were for all year round sale.

Christmas was another busy time. There was holly, cut from a plot of land in Brickhill, to be wired into wreaths at the florist. Boxes of pretty plastic bowls arrived, to be creatively planted up with decorative flowering and leafy plants of our choice selected from the greenhouses.

Judith Kutty

Not posh, half the time we'd be dirt smeared, wet or plant stained. It was hard physical work but I missed life on the nursery and those lovely warm greenhouses that were at the Ramsbothams Nurseries on Brooklands road.

Although only a few years they were unforgettable and very enjoyable.

Judith Kutty

That's so sad: been part of Bletchley for over 60 years, also their nursery between Brooklands Road and Windsor Street, which has been gone for years.

Ken Dobson

My cousin Gordon Alderman worked there for some time. Brother Ron purchased Mrs Ramsbotham's bungalow in Water Eaton Road and lived there for many happy years.

I appeared before Mrs Ramsbotham JP on numerous occasions (in my role as a police officer!). She was a lovely lady.

Terry Foster

My husband's nan wasn't able to come to our wedding. We went to see her in Baisley House straight after the service and later sent her my flowers (also from Ramsbothams). They dried in the heat of her flat and I still have them 54 years later.

Margaret Eggelton

Sad - I remember asking for a single red rose for my wedding bouquet and Mrs Ramsbottom saying I couldn't just have one rose, it would be a bouquet but she'd keep it simple!

It was and it was beautiful.

Sharon Millwood Wildey Roberts

ANGEL'S

Angel Dindol

Between the two upper windows you can see the statue of the angel that was put into the wall. It was covered up later and might still be there. I always remember my father telling me about this store and the angel that was hidden behind the render.

Hilary Smith

In 1931 Angel Dindol draper's shop stood at the entrance to Central Gardens. In the 1950s it was the Central Drapery Store and in the 1970s Mokaris Delicatessen. But by the 1980s it was sadly no more.

Diane McLean

I remember Angel Dindol, run by Miss Whittaker. She did a round with a suitcase of clothes. You could buy items and pay weekly.

I had a look the other day to see if I could see that angel. Sadly it looks like it had been filled in.

Maggie Ash

IRONS

This may stir up a few memories of having your feet measured, or even x-rayed, as Bertie Irons was well ahead of the game.

Behind the frontage

I was amazed to see the raised up seating exactly how I remembered it from the 1950s.

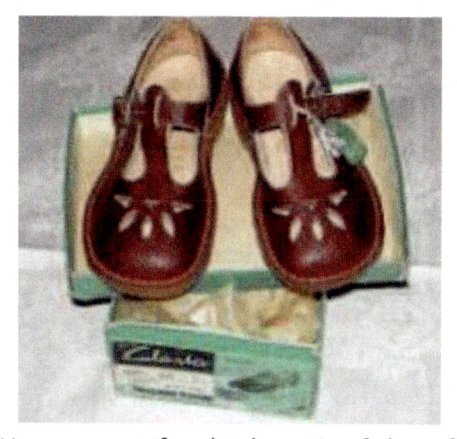

How many of us had a pair of these?
Available in a range of colours - red, brown, navy and white.

Diane McLean

My sister and I always had Clarks shoes. I had very flat feet and had to have my shoes built up on the inside by the cobbler, adding more expense for my parents.

Even the boys wore Clarks sandals when I was young, but only in brown.

Jean Blane Flannery

Mine were red, I loved them.

Ann King

I always took my children to Irons, to have their feet measured for their Clarks shoes. They loved sitting up on the little red tub-like chairs, which were in a row on a platform, and then putting their feet into the x-ray machine.

They wiggled their toes just to make sure that they were looking at their own feet! All part of their childhood memories and my own memories too. As they say, " Those were the days."

Kathleen Roberts

Brown for me and my sister Teresa Sinclair. We even had an open-toed version one year, to see us through to the end of the school summer holidays!!

Jackie Garner

My daughter had them in white for a wedding when she was 4. They looked sweet on her.

Toni Murray

I remember the arguments in there because I wanted platform shoes and my mum would only look at sensible shoes.

Caro Lewis Sanders

Mine weren't the daintiest feet. I lived on eggs and Jersey cow milk, much of the time my feet in wellies. I had a high instep etc so Mum insisted on sturdy, sensible and good quality shoes throughout childhood. She might even stretch the budget a bit for them.

Irons was the shop, foot on the measurement stand to get a good fit!

Judith Kutty

Sun & Summer Shoe!

MINERVA
There's nothing to it but straps! Slim, elegant straps that meet at the vamp and are held at the heel with a snug, elasticised band. A high, Louis heel. In Red, Blue and White calf or Black patent.

unmistakably **NORVIC**

Fit for a QUEEN and Fitting for You

A magnificent selection of fifty different types of Summer Shoes featuring...

Lotus : Delta
Norvic : Kiltie
Clarks : Newmans

A. G. IRONS
X-RAY SHOE SHOP

BLETCHLEY   Tel.: 143

I bought my first pair of winkle pickers there in 1962. I had to save my pocket money for them as Mum wouldn't buy them for me.

Maggie Shepherd

My sister and I were employed at Irons in the early 60s, during our school holidays. We were paid 15 shillings a day plus a small reward if we sold certain shoes! We were told to use the x-ray machine on every child's feet.

Jenny Worthington

X-raying feet was banned after the discovery that the radiation built up in your body.

Richard Larbey

I shudder to think what effect it had on us!

Polly Watts

MARSHALL'S

Jim Marshall was a professional drummer who in 1960 opened a music shop in London with his wife Violet and son Terry, selling both instruments and equipment

The shop soon became successful, patronised by some well-known rock stars of the day. But the amplifiers then available left something to be desired.

Jim and Terry decided to start producing their own amplifiers, which soon became sought after for their quality. The business grew but when the lease on their manufactured premises expired it wasn't renewed. What to do?

One day as Jim was driving up the M1 he saw a sign advertising a factory unit to let in Fenny Stratford. In 1966 the company set up business there and in 1967 opened a shop on Queensway.

Marshall is still a renowned innovator in the music world globally, and still headquartered in Bletchley on First Avenue. There you will also find a recording studio and the Marshall museum.

One thing that struck me is that Marshall's didn't just cater to the serious musician. I wonder how many parents were tormented by the sound of their child's kazoo or mouth organ.

Then there were the recorders - they must have sold hundreds of those to long suffering parents.

Although my lovely wood recorder had a mellower note than the plastic ones, I can't think my own parents were overjoyed to hear me practise on it.

Jean Blane Flannery

I was at Marshall's when it was opened by Screaming Lord Sutch!
Mel Cameron

I bought a couple of recorders and a guitar there.
Becky O'Rourke

The first manager lived in Westfield Road opposite the library and Charlie and I used to babysit his children sometimes. He was a nice guy.

Mary Shaw

I believe Charlie Hill was the first manager of the Marshall's store. I loved going in to listen to records, or just to hang out. There were some great bands that visited.

Alan Jones

I still have my recorder. Every time I come across it I play a couple of random tunes. But it is mostly used these days to attract my husband's attention when he's at the bottom of the garden.

Pauline Madden

I think Marshall's made most of their money selling amplifiers and equipment. But it was an interesting shop.

I remember the torture of my daughter learning the One Note Cha on the recorder.

Later her school let her have a violin; thankfully she got bored rather quickly.

Wendy Gravett

I purchased my first bass guitar from here and went on years later to be the purchasing manager at Marshall's, where Jim used to sit on a drum stool behind his desk.

I still have an unopened bottle of 1998 single malt whiskey. Managers were given a bottle every year.

Iain Tennant

TURNEY'S BAKERY

The smells from Turney's were amazing and probably the reason I became a baker for the early years of my working life, after watching Derek in the bakery. And here he is at work.

I remember the old bread cart was in the yard at the back. Then Derek had a Ford van for bread delivery and I remember sitting on the wheel arch of that with the headlight between my knees on some of the estates we went to, and getting caught and being told off by a policeman about the dangers of doing that.

We delivered to Bletchley Park but of course at the time I had no idea of the significance of it. Now every time I see it I remember pulling up to the front of the house but never being allowed to go inside.

I went with Derek and Rex to the pantomimes at Christmas time, in Bedford I think. Coming back in the dark I used to ask Derek how he could see the road, as I had never been in a car at night .

We also visited an iron foundry which must have belonged to a relative or friend and I was fascinated to see how it all worked.

 Such great memories

I did call In to see Rex a lot of years later but lost touch. Then Derek and Cath died so there were no more Christmas card exchanges.

Derek was a Master Baker of the highest quality and a lovely, kind and generous man always.

Paul Berry, who started this conversation with his post above. Paul went to Bletchley Road School and his dad was school caretaker in the 1960s.

I started working for Derek and Rex when I was about 13. I cycled to the shop to start work for 4am on a Saturday morning, then used to work throughout the school holidays. I absolutely loved my time working in the bake house.

Andy Ward

Derek used to make cottage loaf shape rolls for the Plough at Simpson, when I cooked there.

Marie Love

I remember making those rolls. I used to come to the Plough with Derek. He always took the delivery inside while I sat in the van. He was a lovely guy.

Vernon Leslie Howe

Derek made the most delicious cream doughnuts and strawberry tarts, I have never tasted better. I knocked around with Rex in our teens and we sometimes went back to the bakery for a coffee after the pubs closed - great times.

Barry Linford

My Saturday treat after finishing my paper round was a fresh warm loaf from Turney's. It didn't take long to polish most of it off with strawberry jam.

Richard Bond

My mouth is watering. Years later I often bought a plait from George Ort on a Saturday morning - it never made it home whole.

Diane McLean

Loved his meat pies on early turn!

Terry Foster

Many years ago on Christmas Day my gran used to get the turkey (or it might have been capon in those days) cooked in their oven.

My dad says they used to take it down there early morning before breakfast.

We always had all the family together at Christmas at my gran's little 2 bedroom cottage in Mount Pleasant. Can you imagine about 10 adults and 10 kids in a small cottage?

Jean Fenton

Early morning buses, steak pies, great days!

Mick Coughlan

Before going to Saturday morning pictures at the County it was my job to collect 4 crusty rolls for our tea from Turney's.

I loved those rolls. The crust broke everywhere when you bit into them and the inside was as soft as cotton wool.

Jean Blane Flannery

I used to collect the filled rolls and donuts every morning break from Rowland Brothers timber yard on Simpson Road. The smell was divine - hot donuts and indigestion.

Bernard Bassington

Oh my word, such lovely bread! They used to put an overbaked (burnt) one by for my dad every Saturday. I don't know why he just liked the liked the burnt crust. If you asked him why, he would probably say it put hairs on his chest. Well, it certainly didn't!

Kathleen Roberts

It's really strange but I have always liked a really dark brown, (overbaked) crunchy crust. I have certainly never wanted it to put hairs on my chest though!

Jean Blane Flannery

THE MARKET

We can't leave a shopping trip without speaking of Bletchley Market. Although the general market has moved several times in recent memory, for many years the large market ground was behind Bletchley Road. It was bounded on the other three sides by Duncombe Street, Osborne Street and Oliver Road.

Livestock sales

A cattle market where livestock was bought and sold, and a general market, were both held there. It was also the site of the annual funfair when that came to Bletchley.

There were all kinds of stalls on the general market, from fruit and veg to clothing and bric-a-brac.

Jean Blane Flannery

The market was Thursdays and Saturdays in Bletchley. I'm sure the cattle market was on a Thursday. My grandad used to come over with the cattle and meet up afterwards with the other farmers in the Park Hotel, which was open all day.

Susan Hope Stevens

I remember the Thursday cattle market well. It was on one of these Thursdays that I had to take my driving test and get through all the cattle trucks and shoppers.

Barry Davies

Photo courtesy Living Archive

On a Thursday I used to go to the market during lunch break from Bletchley Grammar and go to the record stall there, where I bought many singles. I remember it like it was yesterday. And yes, the livestock did smell.

Mary Church Hazell

I always walked around on a Thursday. The smell and poo slops etc in the pens were authentic on the day!!!

Pam Tew

I remember those days. We used to go on a Saturday to watch all the cows and sheep come off the lorries.

Jill Elton

I remember issuing animal movement licences on Thursday afternoons, a job usually given to a lowly probationary constable ie me. I seem to recall that it was a warm comfortable job, with tea on tap. Happy days.

Terry Foster

The first Whaddon through Shenley Brook End weekly bus ran on a Thursday morning, returning just after one o'clock. It coincided with Bletchley Market. One later ran on Saturdays too.

Judith Kutty

KNOCKED DOWN IN MARKET

Six-years-old Peter Short, of 27 St. Paul's-road, Bletchley, escaped without injury after being knocked down by a reversing lorry at Bletchley cattle market on Thursday of last week.

He was seen by a doctor and returned to his mother.

From the Bletchley Gazette of 1957

Thanks to Diane McLean for finding this.

After moving to Stewartby, I still went to stay with my Aunt Nellie and Uncle Reg Cutts in Cambridge Street most weekends.

This story is from February 1961. Mum had broken the big bowl she used for mixing Christmas puddings and hot cross bun dough, so I went to Bletchley market one Saturday to look around for one for her birthday.

On a second-hand stall I found a pretty washbasin set complete with large jug and bowl, soap dish and toothbrush holder. I thought that Mum could use the jug for flowers as well as the bowl for her mixing. The set cost the princely sum of sixpence!

Uncle Reg brought it over to Stewartby for me on his next trip to

Bedford buying dog meat for his Co-op butcher's shop. I hid it in my own bedside washstand (not used as such!) until Mum's birthday.

Mum was really pleased with her gift. The bowl made a good mixing bowl and the jug was ideal for the chrysanthemums Dad gave her on their wedding anniversaries. The toothbrush holder made a small vase and the soap dish - a soap dish!

Jean Blane Flannery

The main market seemed to sell almost anything. My grandmother often bought clothes from a Sikh gentleman near the entrance.

There was a pet stall where you could buy a tortoise for 1/6d. We bought one and had it for over 20 years until someone poisoned it.

There was a corrugated tin gents' toilet at the far end and it stank to high heaven - only to be used in dire necessity!

Both markets were very vibrant. The cattle market was fascinating with lots of bustle and shouting, presumably auctioneering and bidding.

Richard Pringle

In the early 1930s my mum was passing a pet stall with my grandad. He picked up a dog for a shilling. Darkie remained a much loved family pet for many years. He is in this photo with Mum and her younger sister Margaret; many will remember her as Marma.

Diane McLean

HOME OF THE CODEBREAKERS

STATION X AND ALAN TURING

Bletchley Park Lake and Mansion

My mum worked with Alan Turing (I am named after him) at Bletchley Park, Station X, in Hut 8 and my aunt in Hut 4.

I knew nothing about Mum's previous history until 1975. All I knew was that she was a nanny to Lord and Lady Cadman.

I believe a new book was written then about Station X and it coincided with 30 years from the end of WWII. Mum and other personnel were not allowed to talk about work there until this date.

We lived in Church Green Road for 27 years and our children were brought up there. They learnt to swim in the lake in front of the Bletchley Park Mansion and played in the grounds.

That is all I'm allowed to say - but I have been in some of the tunnels on training exercises with the Ambulance Service.

Alan Andrews

A SLICE OF LOCAL HISTORY

Between September 1939 and the summer of 1944 Alan Turing lodged at this former public house in Shenley Brook End: The Crown Inn, now a private residence named "Green View."

Diane McLean

Shenley Brook End's one and only pub, originally known as The Crown, was the watering hole at the junction of Bletchley, Whaddon and Shenley Church End roads. It was a meeting place of the Whaddon Chase Hunt.

As school-going youngsters we would see Oil Magnate Nubar Gulbenkien there and sit in his Rolls Royce. But what our parents didn't know was that Bletchley Park's famous code breaker Alan Turing resided here during the Second World War!

The Crown had a pig slaughter house on one end. My dad heard them squealing as we lived just a hundred yards away - but nobody squealed on Alan Turing, even though he cycled and ran to Bletchley and Whaddon.

Although a bomb dropped in the field across the road, it caused no damage to the pub.

The story goes that since Alan Turing was a healthy man, cycling and running everywhere, the Crown's landlady asked him why he wasn't away fighting for his country!

Judith Kutty

Alan's bike was an old, defective machine and every so often the chain would pop off and disengage. When this happened, he had to hop off the bike to replace the chain. On getting to his office, he'd then wipe his hands with a rag dipped in turpentine from a bottle he kept there.

He loved his old bike and legend has it that he chose a tortuous path to devising a solution to the problem with the chain. He eventually discovered that it only happened when a particular damaged link on the chain came into contact with a particular bent spoke. So he simply straightened the bent spoke.

This problem solving approach proves that he was a true mathematician, certainly not a mechanic. A bike mechanic would probably have taken as many minutes to work out the problem and fix it as the months it took Alan!

Jean Blane Flannery

BLETCHLEY PREPARES FOR WAR

Bletchley Park Home Guard

These fine chaps could be a group of the local Home Guard.

My father, based at Bletchley Park and Fenny Repeater Station for the duration of WWII, would have been a member of the GPO Home Guard Unit with his fellow GPO colleagues from Bletchley Park.

Gerald (aka Gerry) is here in his Home Guard uniform with me in his arms, outside our front door. It was about 1944 because by then I was sitting up, as you see me in my pram with my mother Thelma.

Colin Brown

FIRE WATCHING

Among the preparations were the appointment of fire watchers on a number of commercial buildings in Bletchley and Fenny. There was a real fear that a bomb might drop and start a fire that could soon spread and become a real inferno if not quickly put out.

Employees were rostered for duty, a group of them spending the night together on the roof of the building.

My mother started working at the Tetley Tea factory when it relocated to Osborne Street from London. She volunteered to be a fire watcher for the company and always remembered the great sense of camaraderie on those duty nights.

She said it was a lot of fun and really enjoyed those times. The young fire watchers joked and chatted, drank tea (perhaps some at times something stronger) and ate a snack or two to keep them going. But at the same time they kept their eyes open, very aware of the need for vigilance.

They wore helmets, reminders of the possible danger. This image is from WarHat.com, a website that sells headwear and accessories such as the stencil from a number of wars.

When on duty fire watchers also wore armbands stencilled FW and Fire Watcher badges. I don't know what Mum's badge looked like as designs varied between units.

Jean Blane Flannery

My sister was a fire watcher too.

Marie Love

EVACUEES

A party of evacuees arriving locally
Photo courtesy of Living Archive

Some arrived with only the shirts on their backs. Some arrived with what they had tied in a tablecloth or in a battered suitcase. Others brought wealth and started local businesses. It is easy to forget how traumatic it must have been for these children and families fleeing the bombing.

Local people pulled together to find clothes for families that were evacuated and help them in other ways.

There were inevitably clashes but, although there may have been exceptions, by and large the people of Bletchley accepted the evacuees and, after the war, families from the London overspill. The Eggelton family from Leon Avenue, for one, opened their arms and hearts to the plight of others. I know they did not stand alone

One such family arriving in Bletchley was the Kent family. Lila Kent born in 1904, from Essex Road, Islington, arrived with her two youngest children Peter and Marina. Her three older children had been evacuated at the onset of war.

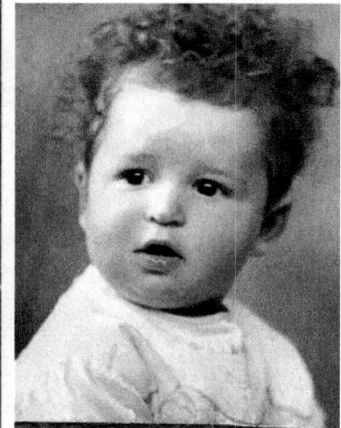

These photos show first Marie (front) with the Eggelton children and then her brother Peter, evacuated with her.

Their father Bill Kent was serving in the armed forces and like so many other young men was away for some years. Marie remembers opening the door to a soldier when she was 5 years old. That soldier was her dad.

Lila worked hard to keep her family together and became a much loved and well-known local character. Her job as a signalwoman earned her a TV slot on "What's My Line." Lila Kent showed true grit and spirit as did so many others.

Lila managed to get a house in Buckingham Road, bringing her family together again.

Maurice Kent, an older son also evacuated at the outset of war, was housed with a lovely couple in Duncombe Street. As an 11 year old he was awarded the Gilt Cross for Gallantry by the Boy

Scout Association. He saved the life of a drowning 5 year old boy who was fishing in the canal.

This notable and brave achievement appeared in the North Bucks Times edition of 12 December 1939.

Maurice may well be remembered locally - one of his jobs was as a projectionist at the Studio.

Marie continues to give back to the community.

Diane McLean

My 2 sisters were billeted for a time in Brooklands Road. One morning when they woke up they found that Mrs Geen's cat had had kittens in the night - on the bed between the two of them!

Marie Love

It was my mother and father-in-law in Lennox Road who opened their door to Marie's family.

A few years ago an aunt sent me a church magazine with a letter from an evacuee who, aged 3 or 4, had stayed with his mother at my grandparents' house. Although so young at the time, he had some photos he sent me.

Margaret Eggelton

My nan and grandad had 7 children and lived in a 2 up 2 down house in Newton Longville. They took in 2 evacuees from London.

The lovely thing is that those refugees kept in touch with my nan while she was still alive. She was 95 when she died, having brought up 7 children and given a home to 2 evacuees. Along with my dad, she also brought up my brother and me - a very special lady.

Sandra Ritchie

I owe my life to a family who kept that connection with the people who boarded their children during the war. The LeJeune's from Fulham were boarded with the Clifton's in Tavistock Street and whilst the family were visiting in 1952 Maureen LeJeune rescued me unconscious from the Denbigh Gravel Pit.

I know at least two of the LeJeune's came back to live in Bletchley later in life.

Doreen Merriman

Our family also had to leave London. Our street was bombed and my parents knew we had to run. My brother stuck a pin in a map. It landed on Bletchley so we headed there. The rest is history.

Kathleen Bairstow

When my parents lived in Railway Terrace they took in 2 evacuee brothers. It must have been a squash with their own 3 children.

Grace Bursac

My nan Mabel Tunks lived in Railway Terrace. She and Mum told me about their little evacuee Arthur from London, aged about 3. I have a vague memory that Arthur's mum was there sometimes.

Beverley Morgan

Joan aged about 9 and Marj (Marjorie) 4 or 5, were evacuees from Chiswick, London. Homed with my aunt and uncle, Reg and Nellie Cutts in January 1941, they lived with them until 1945. They soon thought of Reg and Nellie, and my own parents, as aunt and uncle.

This photo was taken soon after the girls' arrival.

Joan (right) and Marj, in the garden at 12 Cambridge Street with their rabbits, Reg standing behind, and Laddie the dog in front.

Joan and Marj's parents came to visit (by train of course) every few months and brought welcome gifts. I imagine some at least had been purchased on the black market.

Much later Joan told me that those years in Bletchley were the happiest of her childhood. She loved Bletchley and would have happily stayed. She hated going back to London, where she was teased at school about her accent being "posh" and her mum treated her as a skivvy.

Joan remained one of our family, joining in our family celebrations with her husband, until she developed dementia.

See how Marj and Joan have grown!

This photo was taken in March 1945, a few months before Joan and Marj returned to London. Nellie is holding me and Reg stands on the right. I was now 5 months old and the girls loved having a baby in the house.

Jean Blane Flannery

Not such a happy story

My father-in-law was evacuated from Islington as a 9 year old and taken in by a family in Brooklands Road. He remembers living on bread and jam or dripping as the man of the household would use all of his food coupons.

Dave Harris

The Bourn Family and a Night to Remember

We were bombed out when I was three. We came to Bletchley and Mrs Kent, Marie's mum, put us up the first night and then we stayed in the council offices for a few nights. Then we had a little cottage in Shenley Brook End - and then we were bombed out again. I think it was the only bomb that fell on Bletchley.

My mother and my grandfather used to go to London most weekends to bring back what they could from the wreckage. They were very brave, strong people. We loved Bletchley and I had a very happy childhood there.

After a family discussion on being evacuated we found this article, which confirmed that we had rented a cottage in Shenley Brook End after our home was bombed in London.

We were sheltering in a pub the night a bomb was dropped on Shenley, destroying a number of cottages - one of them being ours. Until we found this article we did not remember the name of the pub (The Crown Inn) which is now a private residence.

My grandparents Mr and Mrs Bourn are mentioned in the article. Since finding it I now know the name of the pub and that Alan Turing lived there, which confirms my mother's story.

Norma Chambers

I found the article to which Norma refers in "The Way we Were." This is an extract from the section featuring her parents.

"October 28th 1940 German bombs fell on the village of Shenley, disrupting *(sic)* doing much damage, including to 11 houses.

Mr. and Mrs. Bourn had been having a drink in the Crown Inn at the time. Alarmingly a bomb had dropped not a hundred yards away.

But the experience was nothing new for them. They had been bombed during WWI, whilst living in Hackney, where Mr Bourn had an upholstery business. On the night of September 19th 1940 their home and business were totally destroyed in the Blitz.

Fortunately they had taken refuge in a shelter and the next day set off for Bletchley with their married daughter, the school of whose children had been evacuated to the town. Providing them with assistance, a friend of the daughter met them in Bletchley and from there they then moved to a cottage at Shenley Brook End, which was damaged by the bombs."

Jean Blane Flannery

And here is the Norma Chambers Dynasty, down to great grandchildren.

Diane McLean

OUR CULTURAL HERITAGE

When the clock strikes three ...
... Everything stops for tea

Well, Paddington Bear might be able to say he had afternoon tea with the late Queen Elizabeth II but so too did Bletchley residents the Spence family.

The Queen visited Bletchley 4 April 1966 and dropped in for afternoon tea with Bill and Faye Spence, and their two young sons Colin and Neil, at their home in Warwick Place.

Here's the family, photographed for the newspaper story

Diane McLean

THE TETLEY TEA STORY

Afternoon Tea is big business these days. Drop-in at a garden centre, a posh London hotel or a steam railway centre - the choice is endless and the prices know no bounds.

Bletchley has its own claim to tea-time fame.

The Tetley factory moved from London to Bletchley to escape the perils of bombing and to be in safer premises.

Tetley's was the first company in the UK to sell tea in a teabag. The very first teabag was produced from their factory in Osborne Street 5 July 1953, a day Tetley made history. I write this 5 July 2023, the 70th anniversary of that historic day.

Join me in raising a cup to wish the Tetley Teabag a happy 70th birthday.

Tetley was a British company that was "everyone's cup of tea."

Sadly, with a drop in demand for teabags the factory closed in early 1977 - resulting in more than 400 employees being out of work

Diane McLean

The Tetley Tea company relocated from London to Osborne Street in the early years of WWII at around the time the Premier Press, where my mother was then working, closed its doors. My mother had no problem finding new employment at Tetley's.

The factory was located on the corner of Clifford Avenue, where my dad's brother Bob Blane lived with my Aunt Rose and my cousins Pauline and Janet.

The Osborne Street factory, now housing

My mother worked at the factory until the summer of 1944. She only left because she was pregnant with me. That January Dad had been granted a sleeping out pass from the army and he and Mum stayed with his Aunt Alice in Cambridge. I was born in October.

Jean Blane Flannery

My first job was at Tetley tea factory Watling Street, June 1952. I was a telephonist first then a Powers-Samas machine operator. I stayed there until 1960. You got a pound of loose tea free each week.

Marie Love

Happy Birthday to Tetley's. I remember the packet of loose tea that my dad brought home every week - still drink their tea now.

Stuart Jones

I worked there in the offices for many happy years until they relocated.

Jane Lant

It was my first job after leaving Wilton School in 1959.

Josie Mabbutt

I also worked in the factory, so near our home I can remember running round with a piece of toast!

Gwen Garrett

They used to have tea tasting sessions, where staff were invited up to the tearoom and had to taste various unmarked cups of tea. I remember the manager threw an absolute fit when Tetley came out seventh behind Safeway's own and five other cheaper teas.

"If we can't do better than this, we might as well stop selling Tetley's and stick to producing tea for other people." Tetley Tea came very close to disappearing altogether that day.

Mike Spruce

I have just had a cup of Tetley's. My first job since leaving school was for Tetley's, leaving in 1973. I have stayed loyal ever since (50 years).

Sue Ellender

PEAKE'S

It was in November 1936 that the firm W O Peake Ltd opened its Bletchley factory, concentrating on the production of quality goods: famous Rodex coats - fine coats in exclusive fabrics.

During the war years much of the factory was requisitioned and staff faced difficult times, both working at the factory on the Watling Street and in temporary premises in Brooklands Road.

From the making of Rodex coats the workers switched to making Air Force and Army greatcoats, and then to "demob" raincoats. It was a while before normal production was resumed.

Peake's was a factory which in its heyday offered employment to many local people. The photographs that follow are from the Bletchley Gazette, 9 April 1949.

Groups of women worked at their own tables.

The concentration - Alice Walker intent on making a perfect job!

Pamela Essam models a Rodex coat

Photographs of Harold Wilson show him in a Gannex raincoat. Gannex fabric was invented in 1951 and the first time Wilson was photographed in a Gannex coat was in 1956.

According to the following memories, it would appear that prior to 1956 Wilson actually wore a Rodex coat.

Diane McLean

I worked at Rodex and I remember us making a coat for Harold Wilson.

Maggie Gallagher

My grandma told me that she sewed the buttons on one of his coats many years ago in Rodex, or maybe it was Peake's then.

Margaret McCracken Hogg

"Workers Playtime" was a radio variety programme broadcast by the BBC between 1941 and 1964. Originally intended as a morale-booster for workers during the war, the programme was broadcast live three times a week from a factory or mill canteen "somewhere in Britain." That day it was being broadcast from Peake's canteen.

Thanks to Judi Heavens for finding this photo from about 1957
Diane McLean

If you look at the lady standing by the window here, follow her hand and you can see half a face and eye. I think that is me as they are some of the ladies who worked on the same table as me.
Pamela Essam

I remember listening to the programme at home as a child. Mum had the wireless on most of the morning as she did her housework.
Jean Blane Flannery

My mum worked at Peake's sewing the shoulder pads in coats, and then in later years when we were young she did it from home. She had an old singer sewing machine. I still have her old shears that she had when working at Peake's.

Pat Bateman

Others too have mementos of when they or their relatives worked at Peake's. Here are two.

These are my shears and thimble from when I worked there 1953-1961. I still have to use the thimble when I'm sewing.

Pam Essam

The quality of all the products used, as well as the clothing, was superb.

Wendy Hansell still uses the hanger in the previous photo. She thinks it must have belonged to her Uncle Joe Sheaf, coming to her when his house was cleared after he died.

This too still looks like new.

Jean Blane Flannery

I played cricket for Rodex ladies. Only 1 game eventuated. My brother Joe was in the men's team and he gave me some coaching. But he was so disappointed - I was out for a duck!

Needless to say, we lost.

Kathleen Bairstow

Rodes Ladies cricket team mid 1960s
Photo courtesy of Doug Harvey

My dad (Doug Plum) played cricket there for the Rodexians. The cricket pitch is under Saxon Street.

Guy Plumb

Doug Plumb, Eddie Plumb, Dennis Plumb, who all played cricket for the Rodexians. The photo was taken on Ed's 90th birthday.

Rodex also put on coach works outings for its staff and their families. Here is one such outing, shown in this photo from Kathleen Bairstow.

Jean Blane Flannery

WIPAC

The company resulted from a merger in 1941 of the British subsidiary of the American Witherbee Igniter Company (Wico) and British spark plug manufacturer Pacy, thus forming Wico-Pacy in Bletchley before becoming the Wipac brand we know.

The building's façade was impressive, with the Wipac trademark standing out so contrastingly from the surrounding countryside and its railway-siding background. The firm liked the district and very quickly set down its roots. Its rapid growth was a story of enterprise and enthusiasm, offering employment for many local people.

Like all companies it had an "ideas room." This was a 30 foot square room where a team of six employees was continually trying out new ideas, new developments and new schemes. One such product of which they were extremely proud was a new "oil cleaner," cans of which you can see in the picture below.

Photos in this story are taken from the Bletchley Gazette of 22 January 1949, very kindly provided by Pamela Essam whom many of you know personally and will recognise as one of our "in-house" historians.

Here is a picture of some of the staff, Jake Baker identifying his mother as the young woman second from the left.

Diane McLean

THE RAILWAY

There was a time when Bletchley was known as a railway town, the railway offering employment to many local people.

My dad left school at 14, starting work as a cleaner on the railway and working his way up to become a main line driver. He was not alone in that achievement. In those days working on the railway was a job for life.

Bletchley had a strong railway fraternity. As a young fireman my dad was taken under the wing of two lovely experienced drivers, Jimmy Atkins and Aubrey Goss, who became extended family to us.

My dad, Leonard Arthur Farmer

He was not alone in this. Railway workers from all over town walked or cycled in all weathers, at all hours of the day and night, to book on, carrying bags containing at the very least their "packing up'" and often an enamel mug. If it was the night shift there would be a few rashers of bacon and eggs for the "shovel fry-up."

Jimmy Atkins and Rev Tarbox

The camaraderie of the mess room extended to a few pints shared in the Railway Club and the odd trips to the races were often on the cards

They were proud men who took a pride in their work and in their appearance. Shirt collars were scrubbed, trousers pressed and shoes polished until you could see your reflection in them. I have even heard some stories of hats being groomed.

Let's hear it for the ladies too. Their work and dedication behind the scenes, in the signal boxes and on the platforms, were crucial to the smooth running of the services.

Last of all, let's not forget the wives and the families at home who will have their own stories to tell.

Diane McLean

I can say this now there are no risks! As an 8 year old boy I travelled on the footplate of a freight engine, number 48621, from Bletchley to Swanbourne sidings and back again. My grandad was the driver and Dad the fireman. I can tell you it was hot in that cab but was so good imagining I was the driver, and having a breakfast sandwich made on the shovel. Those were the days.

Graham Baxendale

My grandad was a driver, Bill Dougall.

He loved steam power and would make us laugh telling how he and his fireman would fry bacon and eggs on the shovel, no health and safety rules - or if there were, they broke them.

The drivers would blow the whistle and would wave to family and friends as they passed their houses, concentrating so hard that losing the odd lump of coal down the embankment was inevitable… And of course, it would be a shame to see it go to waste!

My mum Norma Plumb has told these stories of her dad, too.

Guy Plumb

James Atkins was my grandad. My father Ken Parker was also a train driver; he met my mum Eileen through Jim.

As a child I can remember Dad getting his bike out of the shed ready to cycle from Fenny up to Bletchley Station to book on. He always had his sandwiches in a greaseproof paper bag.

The hours he worked were unsociable and often his dinner was left on a pan of water ready to bring to the boil and heat up whatever time he came home - no microwaves in those days!

A lot of railway men lived near us on the trees estate and they all seemed rather good at growing vegetables. They were happy days.

Angie Gray

I was hoping for a lovely memory like this. Many of us will remember the days of dinner being kept warm on a pan of water. And I know for sure your lovely grandad, like my dad, would never have complained: bless them. Also, I think many of us will remember how the railwaymen shared a common love of gardening and that their allotments were often their pride and joy.

Diane McLean

My grandad started as a cleaner and worked his way up to engine driver, and his father was an engine driver before him.

Barry Linford

At least six or seven drivers and firemen lived In Whiteley Crescent, so lumps of coal were commonly found. Though when a great lump of Welsh coal went through a non-railway neighbour's shed and demolished it he was not happy until somebody bought him a few beers in the brickyard club.

Colin Bateman

David was a cleaner, then fireman, then driver. His dad was in Number 1 signal box and my mum, seen here, in Fletton signal box.

Marie Love

My great grandfather and grandfather worked on the railway. The first job for them as boys was cleaning engines, the way so many started. From cleaners they could go on to learn to be firemen and from firemen to drivers.

My grandfather started work in the railway sheds as a cleaner when he left school at fourteen. He lived in Barton then, about four miles from Cambridge, walking to work to be there by 6 o'clock in the morning, then walking the four miles back in the evening.

He progressed to fireman and moved to Aylesbury on the Cheddington line. On being moved to Bletchley, where the family first lived in Railway Terrace, he worked his way up to become a first class driver.

Here he is in his garden at Brooklands Road, where he grew vegetables and kept chickens. A few fruit trees, flower borders and his prize chrysanthemums, were also included.

He was a driver on the Bletchley-Euston run during WWII. And he unknowingly took the last train of the day out of Euston station just as my dad arrived at the platform on a rare leave.

Dad slept on the platform and was able to get home on the early morning milk train. I don't know if it normally took passengers but Dad probably knew the crew.

My Uncle Charlie was also a railwayman, a fireman in 1939, before becoming manager of the railway hostel in Little Brickhill.

Jean Blane Flannery

It was a custom in my family, being railway people, that on New Years Eve at midnight we would go outside and listen to all the symphony of whistles being sounded by the drivers in the Bletchley sheds. If either my grandad or uncle were on shift we imagined it was one of them pulling one of the hooters.

I still even now go outside at midnight for my own few personal moments to remember those long gone - and very occasionally think I can hear in the distance the sound of a train whistle.

Allan Ainsworth

I worked on platform eight in the telegraph office from 1955-1965. My dad Bill Dougall was a driver.

I have a letter requesting that he and Mr Church, Sandy McClarran and Hugh Mackie, attend a training course at Crewe for diesel driving as that was the new way forward. It was signed by Ernie Dodd, loco superintendent.

Norma Plumb

The railway is part of our cultural heritage and many memories have been shared in the group over the years. I am sharing extracts from a story written by Frederick Watkinson. I have chosen his story as it brought a tear to my eye along with raising a few smiles.

10 December 1958 Fred arrived at Bletchley as a passed cleaner on loan from the North West. Fred writes:

"In the North we always used to say "brew up." Another thing I had to get used to was the way of questioning one's parentage. In the North it would result in a punch-up, whereas in Bletchley it was a form of endearment."

Frederick worked on the footplate for ten years before being made redundant and working in local industry. After 49 years of living in Bletchley he retired to Cornwall.

Fred touches our hearts as he writes :

"One has to say that my time on the footplate was the most enjoyable time one could wish for. I had the pleasure of working with many of the parents and grandparents of a number of members of this group.

All of my memories from those days are of the good times we shared and of the fun we had together. Even though at times we had to work hard, it never ceased to be a pleasure to go into work"

Fred highlights the camaraderie and loyalty of the railway men. They were a team in every sense of the word. Fred continues:

"Mind you, some of the hours we worked played havoc with your love life. On more than one occasion I found myself sitting in the sidings at Northampton when I should have been somewhere else. Halcyon days of times gone by."

I'm sure we all agree - a lovely story written to mark the anniversary of the day Frederick Watkinson "Arrived in Bletchley Town."

Diane McLean

THE BLETCHLEY RAILWAY CLUB

In 1956 the Railway Staff Association was given land in Railway Approach to build a club. The building was only a terrapin hut to begin with, until funds were raised for a better home.

My dad Tom Brown was chairman and Bob Mayes was secretary. They both worked very hard to get the club off the ground.

There were a darts club and fishing club. Dancing, Bingo, and Country and Western evenings, were regular events. The club hosted Christmas and New Year's parties for children as well as outings to amateur football at Wembley Stadium, with afterwards a meal and theatre show.

A trip to the amateur football finals at Wembley circa 1952

In 1975 the Association got its own club building on Railway Approach. My father unveiled a plaque on the wall of the new building, placed to commemorate my mother who had died that March.

My mother and other ladies had worked just as hard for the club as the men, including doing the cleaning and helping with catering for various occasions.

Ladies of the Railway Club
Back from left: my mum, Lily Brown, Mrs Bass, Mrs McErlane, Lil Caldwell
Front from left: Kath Weaver, (unknown), Liz White, me, Mrs Bond

The bosses of the Staff Association were regular visitors to the club and meetings were held there three times a year.

Husbands and wives would all go to Blackpool once a year for the big annual meeting for all the Staff Associations, Bletchley being one of these. Bletchley was in fact noted as the best run club in the South of England.

When my father retired as chairman he was made president, a role he held for 16 years.

Tom Brown receiving an award from the Railway Staff Association on his retirement in 1966.

During his years as president Dad ran The Evergreens Club for pensioners on a Monday afternoon. He also organised and enjoyed Bingo evenings on a Monday and Thursday. He continued in this role until the age of 91 years.

The club closed in around 2014, when Bletchley Council bought the land. It was a sad day for my family and many other families. Those days will be remembered as "The good old days at the club."

Kathleen Catalanotto

THE LONDON BRICK COMPANY

When you think of Bletchley, what other thought springs to mind? Surely it is the London Brick Company, part of our Industrial and Social Heritage.

Growing up in Newton Road the brickyard was part of my family's cultural heritage. If the wind was blowing in the right direction we could smell the smoke and see the smuts.

Mum would say it was the "wrong direction" if it was washday and holes were literally burnt in her nylons.

Many of our neighbours worked at the brickyard and we would see them cycle past morning and night on their way to work and on their way home.

They were so tired some days that they would walk into a neighbour's house in mistake for their own, to rest their weary bones. Well, they were tired and the houses did all look the same.

We would see many groups of workers walking along the road from Bletchley and Fenny. We grew up waving to the lorry drivers as they went past.

I have so many fond memories of family, friends and neighbours who worked there over the years.

I will take a step back and let the stories come from members' hearts, anecdotes of the camaraderie shared within the community, an opportunity to pay tribute to those workers loved and respected by many.

Diane McLean

Brickworks entrance on Newton Road, offices to right

There was a railway siding that ran into the brickworks and a signal box on the railway bank about where the houses ended in Newton Road on the Whiteley Crescent side.

I lived in Beechcroft Road and used to watch the trains shunting the trucks when I came home from school.

That steam train smell - any time I catch that smell, I'm right back there watching those trains.

Peter Lubbock

Yes, the brickyard. I remember the Italians from the brickyard sitting on the ground making baskets.

Marie Love

I loved being taken up on the kilns when I was a lad, to see the fires down below. I remember people buying houses in Newton years ago, then moaning about the smell from the brickworks. They saw the chimneys before they bought. Why moan after?

Way Bricks build houses. I think it a shame that not one of the great chimneys was kept as a memory of our local industrial heritage.

John Goss

I totally agree!!! We lived on the Saints estate and could see the chimneys smoking away. I loved the smell of the sulphur and our veg grew wonderfully in the clay soil.

I used to go to tadpoling in the stream at the brickworks. They were good old days, now all gone.

Linda Shadbolt

I remember those days! The smell of sulphur in the washing - I miss that.

I recall arriving at Bletchley train station and thinking it smelt like Bletchley, not realising it was the brickworks I could smell.

Sharon Millwood Wildey Roberts

I remember watching when they blew up some of the chimneys when it was closing down. So many people worked there from our town including my dad.

You knew when it was going rain as you could really smell the sulphur.

Pat Martin

Did we bother about the chimneys back then? The brickworks was a kind of university of trades. Without the brickworks, how could so many houses have been built?

My grandmother and grandfather lived opposite the brickworks in an old cottage and the pits are still called Granny Dimmock pits. My dad and about five of his brothers all worked at the brickyard. My brother Ashley was also there for a lot of years.

The only places to work were the railway and the brickworks, especially if you never had a car.

Maggie Ash

My dad was a brick company employee almost all his working life, apart from his years in the army throughout WWII. He started as an office boy at the Bletchley works in early 1933, still during the depression.

Getting to work he would see a queue of men wanting jobs. The foreman would go out and say to the men, "I'll have you, you and you." Then he would actually say, "And the rest of you can bugger off!"

Dad did about 3 years as an office boy, at the beck and call of the office manager. Then he started to work his way up in the office.

About 1939: Dad 2nd from right with work colleagues, by the office.

There was a boom in the building trade when Dad was demobbed and went back to LBC after the war. He was now working in the Personnel Department and this is what he told me:

"The first people we tried to employ were from Glasgow, Liverpool and Belfast. We would have train loads come in. In the morning they were given a pound and had a night at the hostel. They'd had a day's travel that didn't cost them anything. And in the morning, if you'd got two left to work you were lucky!

Then we employed Polish servicemen. They were still in the army and they eventually went off to places like the mills in Lancashire.

We had the European Voluntary Workers and then I think it was the Italians next. I used to document them all and put them in the hostel. The personnel managers and people went out to Italy and recruited them.

When the building trade was depressed, as happens from time to time, the Italians left for other jobs. That was how we came to have the Indians and Pakistanis, now all round. "

Eventually, after moving to Stewartby and running the Club there for many years, Dad took early retirement in 1980 when Hanson took over the brick company.

If there had been promotion to be gained at Bletchley he would have stayed there, as none of us really wanted to leave - and my own story would be very different.

Jean Blane Flannery

My dad organised the Family Fun days and Mum did the refreshments. I remember the men in the Knobbly Knees competition and the ladies' Ankle competition.

Dad was dispatch officer and was in the Bowls Club. As children we spent most weekends down at the pavilion with our treat of Vimto and crisps. They were such fun days.

Lynda Castle

Not only the brickworks themselves but the brickworks lorries were also a feature of Bletchley. Painted red (Brick Company Red!), London Brick Company Limited written on the side and with George, the hod carrier logo, on the front they were a very familiar sight to local people.

Many of their drivers were also well known local characters. Here is a smiling Arnold Rouse in his lorry cab.

It was a very sad day for many when the brickworks closed, with its loss of jobs and the loss of a local institution. The chimneys coming down really marked the end of an era.

Some of the chimneys proudly standing in years past.

And here is the sad day they came down.

Jean Blane Flannery

If I remember correctly the chimneys came down on a Saturday. I heard a siren go and a few minutes later they came falling down, an impressive sight. It seemed strange when they had gone, when I was used to seeing them daily.

Richard Burnett

THE LONDON BRICK COMPANY SOCIAL AND SPORTS

At one time back in the day, seven brickworks had clubs with their own social and sports sections. While my dad Jack Blane was still working at Bletchley after WWII, he went to Stewartby to organise a Sports Day. Then from 1954 he was employed as Secretary of the Social and Sports Association at Stewartby.

Stewartby was the biggest club, with about 2000 employee members. But the same membership rules applied to every club.

They all came under the umbrella of a Social and Sports Council, to which Dad eventually became Secretary.

In the 1950s and I don't know how far beyond, members paid tuppence (two old pence) a week to belong to their club and the company paid a penny a week for every tuppence.

Clubs had committees to run things but sections had their own committees. The sections too were subsidised to a certain extent.

The clubs also raised money for children's Christmas parties, parties for pensioners and widows too, with events such as whist drives, beetle drives and raffles. All had presents and the company also subsidised these events.

Father Christmas in his long red robe, with presents for everyone.

Bletchley held its own sports day for quite some years, in the sports field off Whiteley Crescent at the junction with Selbourne Ave. I remember going as a young child.

We walked under the railway bridge and down a short track to the sports field itself. In my memory the day was always hot and sunny, and very enjoyable.

Sports Day 1956 Ted Hersee with my dad Jack Blane

Jean Blane Flannery

Sports Day: waiting for the next race

1955 My brother Peter is the dark haired boy on the left and in the top right corner is me in the arms of my sister Anne Wildman.

Liz Jackson

1956 I am having a ride on the switchback, my mum there on the right. Happy days.

Leslie Garman

I have good memories of the club, being in a team for the indoor sports. We played darts, indoor bowling and table cricket. Quite a few teams played. Our team was called the Robins. My husband was in the Electricians team.

Pamela Essam

LOVE IS IN THE AIR

Our journey began 1 February 2023 with the local love story of Ron Ward and Phyllis White, swiftly followed by the blockbuster from Sheila Batham.

With the show on the road we have shared anniversaries, weddings, and celebrated families enjoying quality time together. We have seen brotherly love, sisterly love, and the love shared by parents and grandparents through the decades.

We have shared love stories and seen how romances have blossomed from an early age, from a blind date, from within the workplace, and from youth clubs and local pubs.

Love stories, photos and memories, have been shared by so many. It is very humbling and tugs at my heartstrings.

Phyllis and her father arriving at the church

This picture is of Sheila Batham on her wedding day with her brothers **David, Michael, Alan, Ian, and Malcolm.** leads us neatly into our first story.

Diane McLean

A LOVE STORY

I met my husband Tom on a blind date. Tom worked with a chap called Roger and I worked with Roger's wife Pauline. Their daughter was getting married and we were both invited to the wedding.

Knowing that neither of us had a partner, Roger and Pauline arranged it with us that Tom would come and pick me up and be my escort to the wedding. I was really nervous as I had no idea what he was like or looked like - and I suppose he felt the same.

The day arrived, 29 July 1978. The time for the wedding was near and there was a knock on our front door. So I opened the door and there he stood. My first impression was - very handsome - but I also loved his car, a Blue Ford Capri.

I came from a family that had never had a car so I felt really special.

And here it is - and I'm still smiling.

We went to the wedding. We couldn't talk to one another at all through the ceremony, so we had to wait until we got to the wedding reception. We got on like a house on fire then, never stopped talking.

It got to about 5.30 and Tom said he had to leave as his parents had been on holiday. They were coming home so he had to go and pick them up from the coach station, but he said he would be back. I thought that would be the last I'd see of him but he did come back.

The wedding reception wasn't late finishing so we went to a pub in Milton Keynes village. It was after midnight when I got home. I'd had a fantastic day and we arranged to meet the next night - and every night after that. Engaged 6 weeks later on my birthday, 13 September 1978, the wedding was booked for 7 April 1979.

We put our name down with the council for a place to live and we got a maisonette about 3 weeks before we got married; that's how quick it was to get a place in those days. So then it was a rush to get the maisonette ready - decorating, furniture, etc but we did it.

So 8 months after we met we were married and the rest is history as they say. We have 2 beautiful daughters and this year, 2024, we will have been married 45 years We will be forever grateful to our friends for setting us up on a blind date.

Sheila Batham

A WEDDING DRESS LIVES ON WITH THE MARRIAGE

"Back in the day," when you worked at Rodex your work mates decorated your work table for you when you were getting married That is what they did for Pam Atkins in 1959 when she married her sweetheart, local lad Derek Essam.

One of the decorations was a doll in a wedding outfit.

Pamela Essam used her skills to make a new dress for the doll from the fabric of her own, very beautiful wedding dress.

You can see the lace in the two photos.

Both marriage and doll have lived on for over sixty happy years.

Diane McLean

AN AMAZING ANNIVERSARY

With the permission of Andy Ward I am posting these family photos of his very lovely mum and dad.

Phyllis White can be seen here on the doorstep of 42 Victoria Road.

And here is Phyllis and Ron's wedding group

LOVE IS... A NIGHT AT THE WALDORF FOR £4!

A SILVER anniversary couple are to recreate their honeymoon — at 1959 prices!

Ron and Phyllis Ward spent their wedding night at London's plush Waldorf Hotel 25 years ago on August 8.

Now 50-year-old Ron and 51-year-old Phyllis, of Oakwood Drive, Bletchley, are going back with everything just the way it was — the same room, number 663, for the same money.

Ron, a driver for London Brick Company's Landfill waste disposal unit, payed £3 19s 3d (£3.96) for the night in 1959.

He wrote with the novel idea to the hotel, enclosing his original receipt and key card — and its American general manager William E. Martin immediately gave the go-ahead. Full price would be £82.50.

Ron and Phyllis were married at St Martin's Church, Fenny Stratford, followed by a reception for 60 people at the former Co-operative Society Hall in Albert Street, Bletchley.

They travelled to the Waldorf by steam train and taxi.

"It was like another world to us," said Ron.

"There were thick carpets and everything was sheer luxury. I can remember coming down for breakfast and seeing all the chandeliers.

"I had scrambled eggs and my wife had Dover sole."

• Ron and Phyllis in 1959.

The wonderful Wards — 25 years later.

The newspaper report of Phyllis and Ron's Silver Wedding Anniversary is amazingly romantic, a story to touch our hearts.

Diane McLean

PLATINUM YEARS

My parents, Jack Blane and Kitty Wallis, married 9 October 1940 in St Martin's church. My dad had been evacuated from Dunkirk and afterwards stationed near Sheffield. He was given a short leave for the wedding and a (very) brief honeymoon, which didn't actually happen - but that's another story...

The family group photo from their wedding
Back L-R: Kitty's sister Nellie Cutts, Reg Cutts, Jack's father Charlie
Front: Jack's mother May, Jack, Kitty, Kitty's mother Bertha

For most of the rest of the war Jack was overseas with the British Army. After 1940, he wasn't home again for Christmas until 1945. It was very hard on them both. But he and Kitty hardly spent a night apart for the rest of their marriage.

Married for over 70 devoted years, Kitty remained Jack's "darling" until the day of his death in December 2012.

Jean Blane Flannery

ROMANCE BLOSSOMS IN THE WORKPLACE

I bring you a love story from the 1950s.

My Aunt Margaret Basketfield grew up in Eaton Avenue. She attended Bletchley Road School and was school friends with many of our members or their families

On leaving school, Margaret went to work at the London Brick Company. Like many others she cycled to work every day, passing along Newton Road on her way there and back. Often she would stop on the way home and have tea with us.

Margaret with colleagues at the brickworks

It was whilst working in the offices at LBC that she met my uncle, Kenneth (Ken) George from Stewartby. Their romance blossomed and they married 1 April 1957

Margaret and Ken's wedding. I hand the horseshoe to my aunt.

Once married they went to live in Stewartby, where they both remained for the rest of their lives.

Margaret and Ken

They had two children, Ian and Karen, and lived as a very happy family. The family made and shared treasured memories for many years, even after the children left home.

Sadly, Ken and Margaret have both now passed away.

Diane McLean

THE MARIE LOVE STORY

25 August 1958, Marie Kent sat at a birthday tea table with "the love of her life" David Love and her family. They were celebrating Marie's 21st birthday.

David suddenly produced a key and said, "Here's the key to your house next door." Marie was a bit taken by surprise, even more so when David produced a little red box containing an engagement ring and said,

"That's your engagement ring. We will clean the house when we get married."

Marie was not the only one taken by surprise. Her mum and dad had no idea either. Someone who wasn't surprised though was David's nan.

David and Marie had been sweethearts since meeting at Bletchley Road School. When David was young he would visit his nan in Stroud and produce the lovely photo seen on the previous page from his pocket saying, "That's the girl I'm going to marry one day, Nan." I think you can see why!

15 November 1958 he did just that.

Married at St. Mary's

The wedding group of Miss Marina Joyce Kent, of Bletchley, and Mr. David Royston Love, of Loughton, pictured outside St. Mary's Church, Bletchley, after the ceremony on Saturday.
(BY.115)

Another touching tale told straight from the heart.

Diane McLean

How confident he was of his love for this girl Marie. House first, then the engagement ring on her birthday!

In those times, if Marie had been under 21 her father would have to give his permission before they could marry.

A lovely guy I once knew was met with a shotgun by his girlfriend's father and told to keep away. The young couple did solve things in the end: a "shotgun wedding" of a different kind...

Judith Kutty

THE WEDDING SHOWCASE

This has been one of our most popular and as a consequence I am opening a memory box, putting a new spin on our storylines, now featuring "Wedding Traditions" through the decades.

Diane McLean

The Photo Album

One for the photo album: Libby Marsh with Ray Lubbock in action.

Signing the Register

Cath Merivale signing the register 13 September 1975 at St Mary's Church, with her late husband Bob and Rev Hedley.

Good Luck Symbols for the Bride

Wendy Hansell gives a horseshoe to her Aunt Kathleen Bairstow (née Sheaf).

Marie Love carrying her good luck symbols, leaving the church with her late husband David.

Jojo Thorn hands a good luck charm to Susan Hardy

This is such a lovely tradition.

I see that you can still buy good luck symbols for the bride, so it seems that perhaps Lulu was just unlucky in the person for whom she made hers.

Jean Blane Flannery

It's odd really. I made a very pretty horseshoe for someone a couple of years ago and they screwed their face up. They had no idea what it was about.

Sad when the old traditions sink. I'm sorry I even made the effort if I'm honest.

Lulu Mccoy

Cutting the Cake

Ken Dobson's daughter cutting the 7 tier cake Ken made

6 September 1959
Tracey Thomas' parents cutting the cake at the Conservative Club

The Honeymoon

Pamela and Derek Essam leaving for their honeymoon in Eastbourne.

Colin Brown with his complimentary bottle of champagne

We spent our honeymoon in the Cumberland. It was motor show time as well. I had put my shoes in the corridor outside our bedroom door for the night staff to polish them - as hotel night staff did in 1967! I retrieved them the next morning, put them on, and got a wet foot! Obviously some tipsy joker had come in late along our corridor and tipped a drink, or worse, into them.

After complaining to the management that morning, the shoes were taken to be dried out and we went off out for the day. I remember being in Trafalgar Square that morning, with a full blown Vietnam War demonstration in progress. It was heaving.

Anyway, we got back to the Cumberland that afternoon to be greeted by a bottle of champers, waiting on ice. Happy days.

Colin Brown

This is a story of a honeymoon that never was. My parents married 9 October 1940, Dad having been granted a short leave from the British Army. They had planned to spend a few nights in Northampton, travelling by train (perhaps my grandad pulled a few strings). It doesn't sound very exciting but as newlyweds I don't think they cared where they went.

However, a really thick fog set in and they abandoned the idea. My uncle Reg wasn't going to let their wedding night be boring though.

He made up an apple pie bed, only discovered by Mum and Dad when they tried to get into it. So they had to spend the first part of their wedding night remaking the bed, an unforgettable night for perhaps the wrong reason.

Jean Blane Flannery

This is just the icing on the cake - which I hope will stir up many memories and many more traditions that can be added to the memory box. Remember that every picture tells a story.

Diane McLean

THE WORD ON THE STREET

THE WINTER OF 1962-63

We remember the harsh winter of 1963 and how it affected our day-to-day lives.

Richard and Pauline Burnett play with a friend on Newton Road. It does look cold - see the smoke from the chimneys!

Diane McLean

When the coalmen delivered, my mother gave them a hot drink in a cup and one of them told her he really appreciated it, as they were not usually given one because they had such dirty hands. He was right of course, but she was so kind.

The milkmen also received her kindness. She would wash the empty bottles in warm water before they came, as she said their fingers must be frozen - my lovely mother.

Kathleen Bairstow

I remember walking along the canal towards the end of the freeze and hearing a strange noise, then feeling the ice moving. It was then that we saw ice-breaking barges heading towards us. By heck, did we get off the ice quickly!

Alan Jones

I remember walking to infant school. The snow was over the top of my wellies and my feet were soaked. My sisters and I had to walk to school regardless of the weather; getting a lift was never an option.

The walk was often really hard going after we started secondary school and had to carry heavy books to and from school. It was bad enough on fine days, let alone when we had awful weather to contend with.

The struggle got worse on the days we had Domestic Science because in addition we were carrying baskets of ingredients and dishes as well as our books. I wouldn't change a thing, though.

I remember the coal deliveries well when we lived in Whaddon Way. We had a coal shed and my sisters and I weren't supposed to go in there. Of course we did, and the coal dust always gave us away.

Louise Carey

The water supply froze and the toilets also froze. The gas bottle I was using to heat the caravan and cook with froze too.

I had to melt snow to use for water and had to use a paraffin stove to do everything. This caused the inside of the caravan to turn black with soot from the stove, and condensation ran in streams down the walls.

I lay in bed cuddling my baby to keep him warm.

There were no buses and I was unable to get to the shops for groceries. How I wish I could forget that winter.

Doreen Merriman

I'm sure I was wearing short trousers then. It must have been freezing. In fact I don't remember having long trousers until I went to secondary school.

Cars were not a problem in those days; we didn't have any! We had coal fires in our new council house that had single glazing with ice on the inside. I remember getting dressed for school under the bed covers.

John Sheaf

I remember it so well. I was working at Hemel Hempstead in the railway accounts. We had drifts up our back door and the windows were frozen. I had to get the train from Bow Brickhill to Bletchley, then the train to Hemel.

It was so cold that if you leant against the train window you stuck to it. If on the homeward journey the trains were late and didn't connect I walked home along the A5, knee deep in snow.

Everyone went to work. Now with just a sprinkle of snow everywhere closes down.

Prudence Williams

A couple of things come to mind in relation to the snow of 1963 (at that time I was working on the footplate). I remember one particular week, with George Titchmarsh as my driver.

On the Wednesday we started at 9:40am and were given a parcel job to Northampton via Blisworth - needless to say we got stranded in the sidings until around 11:30am the next day. We were finally released but didn't make it back to Bletchley until around 4:15pm on the Thursday. Quite a long shift!

A second memory is of the time I lived in the railway hostel at Little Brickhill. To keep our social life going, we cleared a path all the way from the hostel to the Green Man so that we could go out reasonably dressed in the evening.

What we failed to take into account was that come chucking out time, we had to leave by the rear exit which we had failed to clear. Sue Bishop took great delight at throwing us out into 3 foot deep snow!

Frederick Watkinson

I was 8 years old and remember sleeping with coats on my bed to keep warm. But I managed to get to school every day. The only heating we had was a coal fire in the living room so only heating in one room. We had a coal bunker in the garden but as we had metal framed windows and doors they froze shut, making it difficult to get out to the coal.

Most of all I remember watching my dad set off every night on his little moped, wearing his greatcoat, and journeying off from Bletchley down the old A5 to work at Dunstable. No such thing as "I can't get to" either work or school in those days.

Iain Tennant

My granny Peggy Basketfield, seen here in her usherette's uniform, also used to stoke the fire at the Studio cinema. Coke would be delivered by the lorry full - no need for sacks, just tipped through the door. Coke tumbled all down the stairs and was all over the floor.

I loved sitting on the dusty old steps watching fascinated as my granny shovelled coke into the stove, which had a massive cast iron door. It was a magical place that was always warm and snug, albeit grubby.

Diane McLean

I was 9 and lived at 48 Derwent Drive, near the blue gates. It snowed, then it snowed some more. We were snowed in totally for 3 days. On the third day a farmer in a tractor managed to get round and gave everyone eggs, milk and I think bacon. Nevertheless Rickley Junior School never closed.

Mark Day-Thomas

HOW WE PLAYED

Whether small town or countryside, in those days it was all our safe playground or perhaps for me walks alone with our dog and my two much younger sisters, as long as we got in for lunch or tea.

But if I hadn't done the allotted household chores or followed the instructions given by Dad for our animals, there'd be trouble!

Eggs and bacon, birds-eye, cow parsley, hogweed, willowherb etc grew everywhere. I wonder how many grow wild in the area now.

Judith Kutty

Kids in Fenny had the playing field, the canal and the river with its wooden plank bridge. The Beacon gravel pit was where we used to swim. The old railway bank up the steps along the Watling Street was a great adventure playground.

A bike ride took us to BrIckhill woods. My, those tyres did some mileage. We were out in the morning with a drink and a snack, our pocket money for sweets, and back in time for tea. We used to nibble the leaves of the egg and bacon plant - tasted like vinegar! Wonderful freedom days.

Pamela Clay

We used to play out (quite a crowd sometimes) in our local area around Chestnut Crescent. One of our favourite places was at the bottom of our street where there was a broad patch of rough land running parallel with the brook, edged by lots of trees and bushes. It was nothing like the tidy stream that's there today.

One sturdy tree had a tyre swing hanging from it. Great fun! But it was the cause of many slapped legs for falling into the brook. We called another tree The Octopus as it had lots of gnarled roots, great for climbing! When the council mowed the grass we made grass hotels. There was also a small car park with a couple of abandoned cars to play in.

There were sticklebacks, minnows, newts, water voles and rats, even swans on the brook. Lovely, apart from the rats. Near the Manor Road bridge was some kind of fenced off power station with some rough land. This was where we found our coloured snails for races. Such fun!

The boys made carts to race down the hill, and sledges for winter. One year, I think it was 1963, we made a proper igloo in Terry Wheeler's garden. There were the ponds down Stoke Road and the Newfoundout. The boys swam in the disused clay pits. There were loads of different wild flowers and butterflies. It was idyllic.

 Once it was late we would return to the Crescent and probably play Sixty Home or something before our mums called us in.

Gina Buckingham

There was a great hollow hedge behind Rickley School next to the Dome, brilliant fun. Also, what was it with all the abandoned cars? Those we slowly dismantled, the back seats then wedged between the chains on the swings to make a double seat - great fun.

Grape Vine

I happily remember roaming the fields around the flooded Beacon gravel pits, fishing and swimming. My pal was Tony Wells from Western Road. But living in Cottingham Grove, we boys mainly used the clay hills and fields at the back of the Newfoundout. The clay hills were obviously made with the spoil, dug out for bricks, from what has become the Blue Lagoon.

There were two steel rails bridging the brook (no sleepers

remaining) that could be straddled to waddle across to the lagoon. The clay pit remaining from the digging was flooded by the overflowing Newton Brook in the winter of 1947.

By the early 1950s when we were roaming there, bee orchids were first appearing, among all the other wild flowers. And when we were older, Bow Brickhill Woods beckoned. My pals in Cottingham Grove then were Tony Smith, Peter Copperwheat, Michael Waller and John Bispham. All have since sadly passed away. So many lovely memories remain, though.

Colin Brown

I remember nature lessons in primary school in which we were taught the names of all manner of wildflowers, insects too. We used to go on nature walks.

I remember that the clay hills had generous clumps of bee orchids, which supported lots of bumble bees. There are quite a few different orchids around the Bluey, plus various rushes. They seem to thrive on the fertile clay-based soils.

John Goss

There must have been many of patches of wasteland around in our younger days. Living in Lennox Road we had the big waste ground behind us (where the library is or was if it has moved) with long grass, weeds, plus a pond etc. There was all we needed to amuse ourselves for hours on end.

Tony Cornes

I loved roaming the fields with my dad, and many friends would tag along as he taught us the names of the flowers and trees. Dad was a real country boy.

Diane McLean

The Gravel Pits were really popular at the weekends. The sandy beaches were a delight to many young families. As for the water, well as long as parents were around to keep watch it was great fun.

Gravel Pits 1957

It could be dangerous though if you were to stray into deep water. My youngest brother did just that and nearly drowned. A neighbour of ours spotted him first and jumped in to get him to safety.

My brother was only five years old and small for his age; a doggy paddle was all that he could do. After this though, he learnt to be a very good swimmer. There was a lot of fun to be had in the Pits.

Kathleen Roberts

We used to go tadpole catching and newt catching. We would watch the tadpoles develop from the frog spawn in jam jars then return them to the ponds. Happy Days.

Terry Foster

What games did children play in Simpson Road back in the day? Glyn Lewis and his friends spent a lot of time fishing in the canal.

Glyn was allowed to do this with parental consent but his mum drew the line at swimming in the canal as she thought it very dirty and very dangerous. That was justifiable as on one occasion Glyn's dad had to pull a local lad to safety.

Trolleys were a much coveted possession and Glyn's trolley built by his gramps was an ace racer. He'd take it down Staple Hall Road at a rare turn of speed. Here he is with his mum and the much loved trolley, a champion vehicle.

Glyn has fond memories of crossing the railway line with his mum's words ringing in his ears: "Don't you go near that railway line."

Simpson Road Railway Crossing

He enjoyed playing football and exploring with other lads, fearless as they entered the confines of Rowlands wood yard, climbing inside hollow trunks and making dens.

Saturday mornings were often spent at the County Cinema.

Diane McLean

I remember when I was a kid, having just moved from London to Bletchley and living in St Catherine's Avenue, I used to go to the London Brick clay pits where I would find dinosaur teeth and other large fossils too heavy to lift.

Years later when one of my kids was doing a project on dinosaurs I took them there so they could find some things for their project. To see it had become a landfill was to say the least disappointing, especially because of the treasures that lay beneath, undiscovered.

Kenneth Higgins

I remember The Plough Inn Water Eaton, fondly, living nearby as a child. My Welsh and Irish grandfathers both loved that pub!

I remember once returning beer bottles to the publican, Mr Fairie(?) and getting the cash deposit given me. I noticed Mr Fairie put the bottles in a box round the back of the pub.

With all the cunning of a young lad, I nipped round the back and retrieved some bottles - then tried to get the deposit back again! Of course, Mr Fairie was not deceived and gave me a talking to. Fond memories!

Bernard Roberts

When I was 3 my parents gave me a penny to keep me occupied while they moved house next door. It gave me an excuse to speak to everyone who went by. I would hold out my hand and say, "Look, I've got a penny." People were very pleased for me, that is until a big boy stole it.

Years later I saw him in a local pub (I never forget a face) and told him the story. He bought me a drink. Did I get my money back? I think it was about 20 years later so maybe someone can do the maths.

Gina Buckingham

I was always sitting making daisy chains with my neighbour and playmate Marlene in the beautiful hay meadows of Loughton. What sacrilege it was for MK to cover them with concrete.

It's strange but I still think about how they took away all our childhood memories and I'm 80 this year.

Josie Mabbutt

ALL THE FUN OF THE FAIR

From being a littl'un through to my teenage years I went to the fun fair in Bletchley. It was marvellous if the weather had been good. However if it had rained, what a mess with thick mud all over. It never stopped us going though.

My dad was a crack shot. He held the armoury certificate for the town, so each year he would tell the chappie on the rifle range to set the sights properly, always with the same reply, which I'm too much of a lady to repeat here! Regardless, dad always won the prizes. He never took them, just did it for the "craic." He was Irish.

The best fair (though the same one), known as the Bletchley Show, was down on the Manor Fields on August Bank Holiday Monday. Later the carnival was held there too. A whole host of other things also went on that day There were field events, a gymkhana, and exhibitions in the pavilion where in the evening a dance was held.

In the mid 1960s this annual event was moved to West Bletchley for a few years, to be returned again to the Manor Fields for a while in the 1970s. Good memories from another time in life.

Kathleen Roberts

The arrival of the funfair on the cattle market was a great summer treat. For a young child in the late 1940s-early 50s it was very exciting with the rides, the stalls and sideshows, lights, noise and crowds. And don't forget the candyfloss! I loved it.

Dad often won a coconut at the coconut shy. When we got it home he made holes through the "eyes" and poured out the coconut milk, which we drank. Dad then split the shell open with a hammer and we ate the flesh over several days. It was a rare treat.

Surprisingly, goldfish won at the fair (by hooking a bobbing duck) and carried triumphantly home in a plastic bag of water, survived. We had two, in a gallon glass barrel that even had a bung at the base. The goldfish seemed fine in there with strands of weed and a daily sprinkle of fish food.

Jean Blane Flannery

I remember the dodgems at the fair, with "Yellow Polka Dot Bikini" blasting out as we went around.

Lynda Castle

I remember going to both the fair and the circus in the market field.

Doreen Merriman

I remember going to the fair and the circus. Bletchley was such a great place then and I am so glad we have those fond memories.

Neil Tomlinson

1978 Bletchley Show in the Albert Street field

My son Jamie centre back on his dad's shoulders, I think watching an entertainer diving/falling from a great height into water.

Joy Doyle

ON THE STREET WHERE YOU LIVED

RAILWAY TERRACE

An aerial view, just showing the railway bridge into Bletchley at the back far left.

Railway Terrace in the background, seen from Station Approach

My memory of Railway Terrace is down to the people who lived there in my young years and teens. If it wasn't for them there would be no fantastic memories. It was a community within a road.

Everybody helped one another, from the gardens at the front which backed on to the railway and where people kept chickens, rabbits or grew flowers and vegetables, to the turning at the bottom which backed onto the old carriage shed where us as kids played football, cricket etc.

Yes I loved that place, where I was brought up from my young years through to my teenage years.

The names I remember of families that lived there, starting at number 1, are the Kershaws, the Bardens, the Mcevoys, the Murdens, the Pitkins, the Dyers, the Wyn-de-Banks, and the Vosses in the last house - number 20, before the turning circle at the bottom. There were others but I honestly can't remember their names.

Railway Terrace was a great place to live and be brought up, from the access alley at the back that led to Cleaver's the building merchants, where we climbed into their back yard while playing hide and seek, to the woods at the top over Buckingham Road where we built camps.

The camps were later all knocked down to build Sherwood Drive and the police and fire stations. But those were the days, happiness in all respects.

Graham Baxendale

Mum lived with a family in Railway Terrace when she first came down from Scotland. I think the name was Esson.

Ann Cornish

My Blane grandparents had eight children, 7 boys and a girl. Their two eldest sons, Charles and Henry, were born in Aylesbury. In 1908 the family, including my grandmother's own grandmother, moved to 9 Railway Terrace, where Donald and Robert were born.

1913 My grandmother at the front of number 9, with her four sons, her own grandmother looking on. Bob obviously moved his head!

By January 1914 when their daughter Margaret was born, the family had moved to 14 Brooklands Road.

Jean Blane Flannery

That must have been next door but one to the Culley's, my grandparents and great granny at number 11.

Angela Evans

According to the 1911 census my grandparents Rose lived at number 19, with 6 children. In 1921 they lived at number 5 with 7 children, 1 granddaughter, and 1 visitor. Those cottages must have had rubber walls.

Barry Linford

> **Bletchley Lad Mentioned in Despatches**
>
> L./SGT. LEWIS WALLER Eldest son of Mr. and Mrs. Waller, of 1 Railway Terrace, Bletchley, now serving in India, has been Mentioned in Despatches, for gallant service in Burma. He joined up at the outbreak of war, having previously been a member of the Territorials. In the early days of the war, he was in France, and went through Dunkirk.

Another name from Railway Terrace: Lewis Waller made his family proud.

Photo courtesy of Graham Baxendale

DUNCOMBE STREET

December 1959 Duncombe Street can be seen beyond the train

Many stories have been shared of Nick Kourdoulou, still remembered fondly.

Some remember walking in for a "short back and sides" without any fuss at all and being asked if they needed a "little something" for the weekend. Nick sadly died of a heart attack in 1981, at the very young age of 56 years.

Diane McLean

Nick Kourdoulou was known affectionately as "Nick the Greek" and ran a men's hairdresser's in Duncombe Street. My mum took me there to get my hair cut in the late 1950s.

I remember him as a jovial bloke and loved to see him singe the hair ends with a lighted taper when he'd finished a cut.

His barber shop was next to the Flyover Café where we used to go from the grammar school at lunchtime to smoke and play on the pinball machine.

Steve Cobham

> **For your individual hair style, visit —**
> # NICKY'S GENT'S HAIR ARTIST
> SPECIALISTS IN CHILDREN'S & GENT'S HAIRCUTTING & STYLING
>
> Open: Monday to Friday, 8.30 a.m.—6.30 p.m.
> Saturday 8 a.m.—5.30 p.m.
> Half-Day Wednesday 8.30 a.m.—12.30 p.m.
> Lunch 1 a.m.—2 p.m.
>
> **Nicky's, 6 Duncombe Street, Bletchley**
> TEL. BLETCHLEY 4189

My parents helped him set up the shop. I remember my mother giving him a trinket box to use as a till.

Peter Nunn

We lived at 17 Duncombe Street. He cut my hair as a baby. And I used to pretend to give my mum a haircut, said it was "Doing a Nicky."

Kevin Garrett

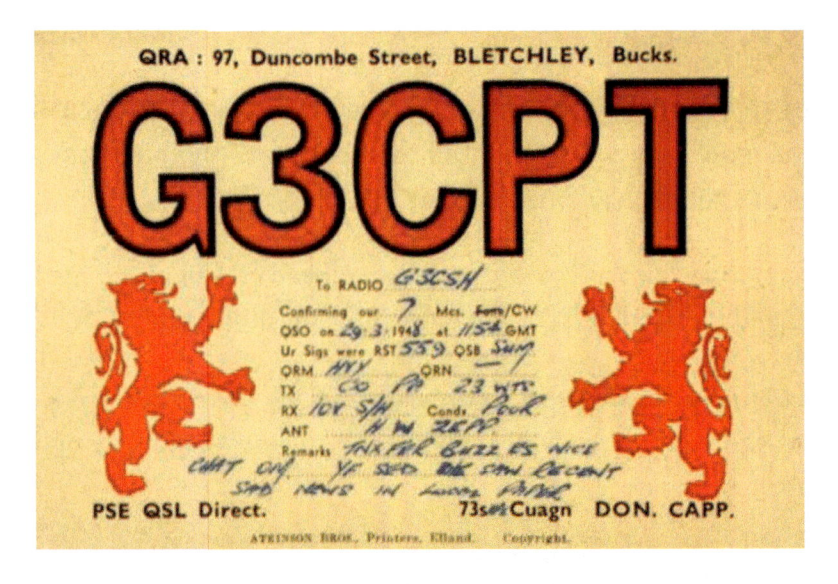

> **QRA: 97, Duncombe Street, BLETCHLEY, Bucks.**
> # G3CPT
> To RADIO G3CSH
> Confirming our 7 Mcs. Fone/CW
> QSO on 29·3·1948 at 1154 GMT
> Ur Sigs were RST 559 QSB Sum
> QRM ANY QRN —
> TX CO PA 23 WTS
> RX 10V S/H Condx Poor
> ANT H W ZEPP
> Remarks TNX FER QSO ES NICE CHAT OM. YF SED NR STN RECENT SBD NEWS IN LUCKY PAPER
>
> PSE QSL Direct. 73s & Cuagn DON. CAPP.

The previous photo is of a radio ham calling card postcard of an operator living in Duncombe Street. It's dated 1948 so I don't think I'm treading on anyone's toes!

Nick Halewood

This photo was taken outside our house in Duncombe Street, where Sainsburys car park is now. I'm holding the pram, my cousin Ian Thompson sitting in it, my cousin Julie on the wall.

Ken Dobson

Doug Harvey's family in Duncombe Street

WESTERN ROAD

My nan and grandad lived at 155 Western Road.

Although Grandad died early, my many times staying at 155 mean that even today I can describe the whole house, from front door to garden and upstairs, far more than any of the four houses I lived in with my family in Bletchley. The frost on the inside of the windows, metal frames, in winter meant you got downstairs quickly once up from the goose feather eiderdown on the iron bedstead.

Barry Hardwick

Were it not for Western Road I wouldn't have been born. In WWII my dad was billeted at number 68, home of my mum's sister Bet Rodway. The house is still in the family.

Dad had moved from Cheshire and was in the Royal Signals, working from Hanslope Park for the MOD. My mum was at Bletchley Park and lived at my grandad's farm in Great Woolstone.

Her childhood sweetheart, the local vicar's son, was tragically killed when his Lancaster was lost over the North Sea. Only 19 years old, he'd asked his new friend to look after Mum if he didn't come back. My dad honoured his wish and married my mum.

Jill Jorgensen

Behind our garden at Western Road was an area of overgrown waste ground, a child's delight. A short track, a little distance down from our house (on the right as you went towards Cambridge Street), led back to this waste ground.

As you entered the area there was a big pond to the left, an old gravel pit with overhanging trees where we would climb and play. We climbed up into the trees, right out over the water, but I don't remember anyone ever falling in.

Either side of the track were beds of stinging nettles. These were not so good!

I was on the track just getting used to riding my bike when guess what? I hit a bump or something (or nothing!) and off I went into those nettles. That was no fun at all. But at least dock grew by the nettles.

Here I am in August 1953, sitting at the end of our garden, our dog Bess next to me. You can see the waste ground beyond the fence.
Jean Blane Flannery

My grandad's house backed on to this small pit, We'd walk over to Tavistock Street, under the railway bridge and over to the big pits at Beacons.
Steve Varney

I vaguely recall some of the scenes, but maybe a few years later. I visited my nan who lived on Western Road. My aunt, uncle, brother and eldest cousins were all about the same age. We played in the air raid shelter in the back garden with lots of kids of around the street. Fun and games, it was freedom for my brother and me coming down weekends from London.

Maureen McCotter

I used to play in that air-raid shelter when I was young.

Margaret Davis

I remember 126 Western Road well. I remember decorating the old shelter, then everything falling off the walls because it was so damp. Mrs Stevens lived next door, then Mrs McGee.

I always thought it was the longest road in Bletchley, so cold to walk up in the winter.

Molly Mccashin

My dearly beloved dad Len Farmer in the garden of 92 Western Road, checking that my cousin Tina Thomson and me are enjoying our treat. I have since learnt it was my second birthday, many moons ago.

Diane McLean

OXFORD STREET

As a child, Bletchley was the centre of the universe! Growing up in Oxford Street next door to my paternal grandparents (incidentally the house where my dad was born), was as idyllic as life could get.

In the garden with my much loved grandparents

Back in the day when playing in the street was the norm, roller skating or go-karting down St Martin's Street were two of my favourite pastimes.

Also among favourites were skipping, hopscotch, French skipping, five stones (jacks) and spending hours over the Co-op fields. Accessible from the Co-op fields, if you climbed over a chain link fence, were Mr Meuleman's apple trees.

When the trees were heavily laden, it has been known for a couple of us to help ourselves to a few apples. I believe this was called scrumping. Surely Mr. Meuleman couldn't possibly eat all those apples!

I spent many happy hours accompanying Poppy Dick (my paternal grandfather) to his allotment or to spend time round his older brother's house in Sandringham Place. Great-uncle Jimmy had an enormous garden where he grew fruit and vegetables, and kept chickens.

As I grew a little older, swimming in the Queen's pool and visits to Leon rec were added to my "playlist," alongside being allowed to ride my mum's bike on the road! Children of my generation were easily pleased.

My dad didn't own a car so we travelled everywhere by bicycle, train, bus or shanks' pony. I knew nothing different and didn't really feel that I missed out.

On a Sunday afternoon we had bike rides to Brickhill woods or a walk along the canal towpath, often culminating by stopping off at the King's Head (Watling Street). There I had a glass of lemonade and a packet of Smith's crisps, with the small twist of blue greaseproof paper containing a sprinkling of salt. What a treat!

From the age of eleven or twelve, I started volunteering at Bletchley library. On leaving school aged 16 I secured my dream job of library assistant. With hindsight, this was the best job I have ever had.

In my teens, the highlight of the week was attending the youth club at St Martin's Hall. To this day, if I hear "Money" or "Build Me Up Buttercup," I'm immediately transported back to that time.

Wonderful memories from when life was simple and, like a lot of our fruit and vegetables, entertainment was homegrown!

Ann Elliott Stephens

OAKWOOD DRIVE

My parents were living in a little cottage in Woodbine Terrace in Fenny Stratford when the opportunity came for them to move into a brand new house in Oakwood Drive, the footpaths not even built. Not wanting to return to Dagenham after the war, their house no longer standing, my mum had made herself at home in Fenny, her sister also living there in Church Street.

Mum in the garden

I won't say Dad was particularly keen to stay, he was a real city man, but hey he wasn't about to refuse this lovely new house. Although still attached to the army with special services, he had a good job as a telephone engineer so no reason not to stay; plus they had Me! (and a baby brother of six months) when they moved into their new home. Mum and Dad eventually moved into a bungalow but Oakwood Drive house remains in the family.

At 3 years old, this seemed to me a huge, cold house. In January 1951 we had a coal fire in the sitting room and a small electric fire on the wall in the small dinette, as we called the dining room.

The two large bedrooms each had a gas wall mounted fire, but there was no heating in the small bedroom, my room from 6 years old. There were a gas cooker and a gas wash boiler in the kitchen, all very mod cons in those days.

In September 1952 we were joined by a new baby brother, and we all three shared the big back bedroom for 2 years. Then it was time for me to have my own room.

Kathleen and her brothers

We had a large back garden, which until we were in full time school was our playground, as were the gardens of most of the children, only then being allowed to play out the front. Our garden was home for many of the neighbours, many of the boys being the same age as my brothers.

I clearly remember looking out of the front window one day with my mum as she spied a lady she used to work with at Bletchley Park. "Oh lovely" she exclaimed, "It is Kath Henshaw" (her maiden name). Mrs Kath Davis was indeed moving in across the road, and best of all for me she had a little girl. Pamela was just a bit older than me and we became good friends once out of the garden restraints.

Almost every house in the very long road had children. Age groups were formed and little groups of us ventured down to Manor Fields. We knew our boundaries, one of them being not to cross the rickety bridge which accessed the A5. We were forbidden to play along the canal bank - well as if we would!

There were two nearby recreation grounds, one off Sycamore Avenue and one in Oakwood Drive. Street games were fun and the lack of cars on the road meant we could run across, just standing back for the odd bicycle.

Several youngsters went fishing with their dads along the canal. Our immediate neighbour Frank Worby took his sons and got my youngest brother interested in fishing by inviting him along.

We all attended Manor Road Infants, moving on to Water Eaton Road Juniors. And once we were of school age we all went along to the old County Cinema.

In those days of the 1950s the council mowed the front lawns and the whole neighbourhood was kept in pristine condition. After the mowing we would build dens with the heaps of grass left behind.

The boys often played cricket and wickets were drawn in chalk on the barn walls. Oops! the barn window smashed! Suddenly all the culprits scarpered...

Each Sunday we would be seen in our Sunday best going to and from church, and very few played out afterwards as it was a family day.

Kathleen aged 14

My love of Fenny and the folk who dwelled there will always be with me. Indeed, I bought my own house there after moving from Buckingham Road. I sold it to a daughter in 2001 and now my eldest granddaughter has bought it from her parents.

Much has changed in Oakwood Drive, very few original residents there anymore. However, there will always be something about that road that to me no other has. Would I live back there now? No! Not unless everyone else moved back with me.

Kathleen Roberts

When we lived in Oakwood Drive I had the smallest bedroom in the house. In winter I used to wake up with thick ice on the inside of the windows as it was so cold in there. We had no central heating in those days.

My dad had a great big heavy duffle coat (like the ones you see in old films that the captain of a warship would wear) that was so heavy I couldn't even pick it up. He put it over the top of me on cold nights when I was in bed and always asked if I was comfortable before leaving me, because it was so heavy that once it was on top of me I couldn't move. It definitely kept me warm, though.

Andy Ward

ALBERT STREET

From left: 12,10 Albert Street, Co-op shop.

Number 12 was built in 1887 and 10 a few years later. The Co-op was the last addition. I think number 10, the house my grandparents lived in for many years, used to have a sweet shop at the front.

When the Co-op buildings were demolished sometime after my grandparents had moved, the soap advert was revealed. This picture was taken in 1991.

Lester Kirk

WHITELEY CRESCENT

The train to Oxford passing Whiteley Crescent, taken from the clay bank above the knothole. It brings back happy memories.

Jean Blane Flannery.

I lived at 83 Whiteley Crescent, just oppose the garages and the railway bank. We used to go under the arch to the fields. We paddled in the stream that had a small bridge over, spent the whole day there. We had no "Health and Safety" rules then. And we turned out OK - I think!!!

Pam Tew

It was great growing up in Whiteley Crescent. There were lots of friends to play with and never any problems. We had great fireworks in the rec at the top of the garden with the kids from Newton Road. The LBC club as it was then was great too, especially the family fun days.

Jane Higgins

I lived in Whiteley Crescent, still do, and started at Church Green Road School in 1952.

The following picture shows a group of us kids outside my house in Whiteley Crescent in happy days.

From far left: Derek Claridge, Colin Castle, Jean Rowe, Pauline Varney, Christine Varney, Tina Essen, Rita Sibley, Terry Essen, Bryn Jeal, Margaret Burnett, with back to the photographer Roy Holne.

Moving on in time, the next picture shows me with my dear dad on his motorbike in front of our house in Whiteley Crescent when I was 17 years old.

Tina Jones

In front of our house about 1968

From left (using the girls' maiden names) Donna Halling, Kevin Halling, Ann Halling, me, Betty James (my mum), Jackie Halling, Mona Halling (my auntie) and Bill Halling. I lived at number 85 with Mum and Dad. The Halling family are auntie and cousins.

Ron James

We moved into our brand new council house, 1 Whiteley Crescent, in early 1948. Those houses were really well built and had not only an upstairs bathroom with toilet but another, outside toilet, close to the back door. With its living room, dining room, kitchen and three upstairs bedrooms, my mum loved it. It was my parents' first home of their own, with just me and no other relatives.

These memories are from the summer before my fifth birthday to the age of seven.

The following picture shows me with two of my friends, Robert Smith and Derick Claridge, sitting in front of my house taking time out from our activities. You can tell how new the build is, with no grass covering the soil yet. The paving slabs look pretty clean too!

We all used to wander about and play together. Our parents didn't worry about where we were or see any dangers in our being out on our own. Often we went across the very quiet road and under the railway bridge. From there we scrambled up the clay bank to where we played and looked over the knothole and the navvy digging out the clay.

Mum and Dad didn't know we went up on the clay banks. We all knew that we certainly wouldn't have been given permission! My parents have also since confirmed that - in no uncertain terms.

Another play area was in the hollow centre of thick hedgerows, across the Newton Road. This was a favourite in the evenings as parents could not find us when they called us in.

We didn't leave it too long before going home though, as we didn't want to be in real trouble.

At other times we just played in the crescent.

Jean Blane Flannery

ON THE BUSES

This iconic photo from 1967 of a number 396 United Counties bus tugs at my heart strings. It was published in the Extra edition of the Milton Keynes Citizen, 1 February 2024.

I spent many years travelling backwards and forwards on the 396 and 397 - to school, to Bletchley station, to go shopping, to work, to the Studio, to Water Eaton and Fenny.

Thanks to Merrial Muse we have this bus timetable.

I have fond memories of waiting at this bus stop. Back in the day many BGS pupils would have queued here.

Diane McLean

The 396 was the bus home from the grammar school for me, going through Water Eaton to Fenny Stratford. Getting off at The Plough cost tuppence but to go one more stop round the corner to Manor Road, although it was closer to home, cost an extra penny. No brainer - get off and walk!

Angela Evans

We always used the buses, got on at George Street and off in St Georges Road or Newton Road. The drivers knew us so well that when we got married at St Martin's Church they stopped the buses (all 2 of them) and watched our wedding.

Susan Hope Stevens

When I was in the top class of Bletchley Road Junior School we moved house from Rhondda Close, Fenny Stratford to Whalley Drive. There were a number of "West Bletchley" children who were picked up in a coach at the end of the day but I wasn't allowed.

However, I was allowed to leave 5 minutes earlier with the "bus children." I had to sit on the wall outside the school and wait for the 396 or 397 to take me to Church Green Road, then walk the rest of the way home. I'm not sure I'd let a 10 year old do that these days!

Karen Leggett née Watkins

I remember when I caught the bus to Wilton School in St Catherine's. Coming home I got off in Warwick Road. I know it changed numbers somewhere.

Eileen Neath

The bus changed its number between 396 and 397 at Saint Clement's Drive. This was effectively the end of the route years ago and the bus would pause there for a few minutes. A new ticket was issued if you wanted to continue further.

Brian John Fielder

One day waiting for my bus I was approached by a photographer from the Gazette. He was interested in my purple and silver wedged platform shoes and my Portabello Market Indian print dress - which smelt like a dead camel! He took a picture of my shoes.

I felt I was the cat's whiskers and as I climbed the stairs of the bus I spotted my mum with a friend at the back. I waved and called out to her. She slid into her seat and pretended she didn't know me, embarrassed by my attire.

Maureen McCotter

When we lived at 1 Whiteley Crescent Mum went to visit Auntie in Bletchley every Thursday afternoon. It was a rush to catch the bus, as before I started school we always had to have "Listen with

Mother" on the wireless at 1.45pm. I think the bus must have been at our stop on Newton Road soon after two o'clock, not long after the programme ended. My younger sister Carole remembers being just the same.

Jean Blane Flannery

Buses used to be packed tight back when I lived in Far Bletchley. On market days it would be standing room only.

I remember being 9 months pregnant and living at my mother-in-law's house in Arundel Grove but took the chance to go down to the market. It was alright going but coming home about lunch time the bus was packed.

As I got on the 397 the conductor shouted, "Upstairs!" I said, "Not if you don't want a baby born up there." He looked at me a bit suspiciously so I pulled my winter coat back. Oh dear, he then said, "Make room for this lady please." A man got up and gave me his seat.

My daughter was born the next day on Friday February 18th, the day we moved into a little farm cottage.

Kathleen Roberts

When my sister and I were young we used to bus across Bletchley to get to school. One morning when we were on the 394 going round the corner by the Dolphin pub, the conductor came flying down the stairs and out the door!

Being the only two on the bus we had to go and tell the driver that the conductor had just gone flying off the bus. I think he thought we were joking until he saw the conductor running up Whaddon Way after the bus. It still makes us giggle now.

Karren Saunders Smith

Another well-used bus stop

Frank Smith came down the stairs as Stan Young was turning into Church Green Road by the 8 Bells. Poor Frank ended up on the road! This was a 60 seater bus with an open platform at the back.

Mick Coughlan

Elsie and I had been dancing at Whaddon Way. We got on the bus in the pouring rain, only us two on it.

Several passengers were waiting for the bus when we arrived at Bletchley bus station. But the driver locked the door, unrolled a little mat, laid it down, and prayed.

Elsie and I cracked up. We were hostages! The customers outside were not happy.

Marie Love

My 1st wife lived in the close halfway along St Clements Drive. I used to catch the 10pm bus which lay over for a short time at the St

Catherine's Avenue junction. The crews would wait until I was 100yds from the bus, then roar away into St John's Road.

They then waited, roaring with laughter, at the next stop for me to climb aboard puffing and panting.

Lovely Heather Smith and Terry Cronin are names which spring to mind. Heather later became a Traffic Warden and Terry joined Bucks Police in due course. He was my crewmate on Traffic.

I would meet John Castle on the bus, hopping off at the Working Men's Club for a pint and a game of snooker. Happy Days!

Terry Foster

Many years ago, I was on the bus one Friday evening going to Fenny from St Andrews to visit my mum, my then 2 year old youngest daughter on my lap.

I paid my fare but instead of putting my purse back, as I thought, into my handbag I must have dropped it between my daughter and the bag. So on arriving at our destination and alighting from the bus the purse, which contained my week's housekeeping money, fell unnoticed onto the floor.

It was only after arriving at Mum's when I looked into my handbag for something else, that I discovered the loss! Help!

I rang the bus station in the hope that the purse had been handed in. It had! Heather Smith was the conductress and as it was the end of her shift she had checked the bus for lost items and had thankfully found my purse. After that episode I always made sure that I looked at what I was doing when on the buses.

Kathleen Roberts

Working on town service in the North East the last bus was about 11.00pm, after closing time for the clubs and pubs. I would stand at the back trying to stop the drunks falling off. Much more civilised passengers in Bletchley didn't give me this problem.

I loved working "on the buses." When I began in the North East it was just after the winter of 1963. I was issued with a big thick overcoat and warned that it was possible that I may have to spend the night in the bus in the North Pennines. This had happened to some of my work pals just a few months before I started work. Buses still ran in the North East whatever the weather.

Doreen Merriman

I remember that the bus depot was just round the corner in Tavistock Street from me when I lived in North Street. Reg Ward was a driver and his wife Joyce was a clippie.

Tony Slater

A smiling clippie - Ding! Ding!

I was a clippie in 1966. What got me was that when we cashed up the money was all in ha'pennies. I never did understand this.

I lived in St John's road then and the last bus stop on the route was 100 yards from my house. If I was on the first bus in the morning I had to go to the garage in Tavistock street to get on it.

Anne Falcus

These badges belonged to John Meagan, Yvonne Gilchrist's dad

In these buses, drivers were in a cab shut away from the passengers. The buses were open backed with a pole to help passengers embark and disembark.

When I moved to Bletchley in 1973 I could not believe the bus service by United Counties!

They operated from the Leisure Centre and often missed stops around the Queensway area. Conductors dressed in casual clothes and the windows were so dirty you had to ask the conductor to alert you when you reached your stop.

On hindsight though, these were happy uncomplicated times and I can only smile at what we put up with in those bygone days.

Linda Milson

I remember when I was a child, waiting with my mum on Newton Road for the first double decker bus to come to Bletchley.

Pat Martin

I just loved to ride these buses with my mum and would often ride from George Street (where the buses started back in the day) to Wolverton. It was such a nice ride through the country side, sadly not anymore.

Martin Wright

Once as I was getting on a bus the driver was John Halsey, who had lived in Church Green Road. I said, "Hello John," and he asked me who I was. When I told him he said, "I thought you were dead!"

Pamela Essam

We lived in Shelley Drive. The 396 dropped us off at the Co-op in Newton Road. If we were going into town, we caught the bus outside the old wooden Sunday School building opposite.

Stella Wells "Riches"

I used to hope it was my dad driving the bus so that we could wave to him when we were playing outside our house in St George's.

Joy Whitten (Shipton)

We've had the 395 and 396, possibly the 397 outside Cramphorn's, so here's the 394 to complete the set.

HORSES REMEMBERED

Many of our parents and certainly our grandparents will have grown up with deliveries by horse and cart being a part of everyday life, the "rag and bone man" a familiar sight.

Diane McLean

A friend of mine was terrified of the rag and bone man. She thought he was called that because he was made of rag and bone. When she heard him coming she ran and hid. He gave her nightmares throughout her childhood years, even after she knew the truth.

Jean Blane Flannery

My paternal grandfather was born in North Crawley, the son of a gamekeeper, and raised in a rural community. My poppy, Fred Elliott, often told the tale of walking a horse to market in nearby Bedford (ten miles away), rather than riding it.

This would result in the horse looking "fresher," thereby achieving a better sale price!

Ann Elliott Stephens

My paternal grandfather was born in Quainton, just this side of Aylesbury, and his father was a herdsman. My maternal uncle was a gamekeeper. My maternal grandmother was born and raised on farms, which would have had horses, in what was then a much bigger Fenny Stratford.

My uncle used to teach us so much about wildlife when we were small - perfect for "Pointless."

Gina Buckingham

Outside the Eight Bells in Buckingham Road
Photo courtesy of Stuart Breedon

My father's family, like many more in those days, didn't go away on holiday when he was a child. But every summer there was the annual Sunday School outing in a horse and cart, a rare treat even though just to somewhere fairly local where they could picnic.

Dad's first job when he left school in 1932 was on a horse-drawn Co-op milk float, ladling milk from churns into the containers of the those making the purchases, usually housewives.

The milk in those days was all unpasteurised, full fat and unhomogenised, the cream rising to the surface.

The children probably rode in a cart like this on their Sunday School outings.

A Mr Baker lived in a thatched cottage in Church Green Road. He had a field next to Holne Chase School land, which is now part of Cottingham Grove. There he kept horses and donkeys that he took to all the fetes as well as other places for people to ride.

Pamela Essam

A Grammar School fête, where we believe these are Mr Baker's animals. A very young Dave Harris is the blond rider far left.

The Owen brothers were always down there and every year Bella dressed up her massive Arab horse for a show. But to be honest, when he cantered up to the gate I was scared of him because he was huge.

I also remember taking wild flowers to Bella when she was poorly.
Josie Mabbutt

British Railways had a number of horses that worked specifically for them. Horses were used for delivering goods and for shunting.

I haven't been able to discover where the local work horses were stabled or who had responsibility for them at Bletchley or Fenny Stratford Stations.

The next photo is an action shot. It was taken in the 1930s but I believe horses continued to be used by the railway companies and then British Railways until the 1960s.

Diane McLean

Charlie and Butch were the last of the shunting horses to work for the British Railways network, retiring at Newmarket station in 1967.

Judith Kutty

The railway dray from Station Approach was horse-drawn but my fading brain cannot recall the drayman's name. I would scrounge the occasional lift to school when lucky. The dray was replaced by a 3 wheel Scammell.

Terry Foster

My dad Ernie Barnes drove the horse and dray, Scammell and occasionally the maroon horse box at Bletchley station from the late 1940s to 1954.

Paul Barnes

There was a horse at Wolverton goods yard, used for shunting the wagons into the shed via the wagon turntable.

John Bowler

Bill King became the locomotive shed blacksmith in 1914. When he started work there, eight railway horses were used at Bletchley.

Being trained for shunting work in the station area, the shunt horses were kept in stables next to Railway Approach. There were also stables available for passengers to leave their horses when taking a trains journey.

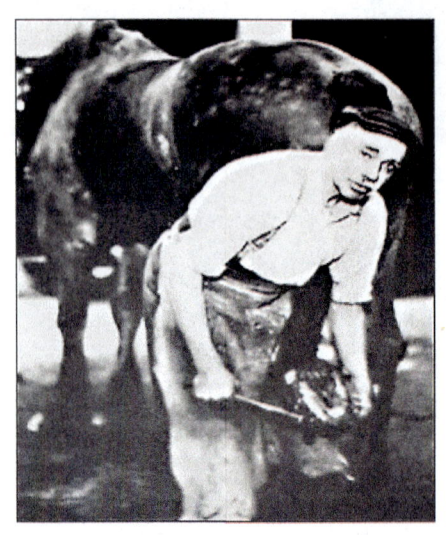

Bill King at work

My dad's younger brother Martin, the youngest of the Blane children, was born in 1920. This is his memory of Bill King.

Drivers had a round tin with their number on it where their pay was put. I went down on a Friday to collect it if Dad was booked off. Then I'd go and watch Bill King the blacksmith. He had a lot of work to do because the railways used heavy horses for shunting and he made frames for firing the locos as well.

I sat on a stool by the forge. Quite a few men came in for a good old yarn in the cold weather, sport or anything, taking the mickey.

I got on well with Bill King. He knew my dad Charlie and my oldest brother, another Charlie who worked on the railway.

Everyone knew everyone else in town, you felt part of a community.

THE PASSING OF STEAM - THE END OF AN ERA

We remembered the era of the regular use of working horses, including those on the railway, in the last chapter. It seems appropriate now to close this book with a story of a later ending, one that many of us will remember and that truly was the end of an era. That steam trains in America were originally known as "iron horses" is perhaps fitting.

This story is taken from notes transcribed from a treasured tape recording of Bob Merivale's memories, kindly made available to us by his family. It is very poignant to me. My dad took this same journey as did so many others. We pay a tribute here to Bob and other railwaymen of that era.

Bob was Bletchley born and bred, starting life in the cottages by the old Shoulder of Mutton. On leaving Wilton School in the early 1960s Bob joined the British Railways as it was then. He worked for the company until the days of steam were no more.

Bob aspired to being an engine driver and was delighted to secure a job cleaning steam engines, the first rung on the ladder, at the princely wage of £3.13/6d a week. That was comparable to other jobs at the time.

After passing a stringent medical, he was thrilled that he "was legitimately allowed to touch steam engines - no more sneaking around the loco sheds."

Armed with overalls, gloves and clogs, Bob was ready for some action. His jobs involved replacing damaged fire boxes, as well as working with steaming boilers and embers that were still glowing red hot. Looking back, he recalls it being quite a nightmare. There were no Health and Safety regulations. You could even skate on the grease that was thick on the floors, not a job for the faint hearted.

Bob worked regular weekday shifts and Saturday mornings, having the time of his life alongside other like-minded lads. They were young lads having fun.

All of them had the ambition to become firemen eventually, after starting with this lowly work. And all of them would go into the station on their days off to see the engines.

Also fondly remembered was some "tom foolery" that went on in the loco sheds. Passing the metal staffs was always a good one, laying the field wide open for practical jokes.

When out with the drivers, if ever the train hit a pheasant the driver would stop the train and say, "Go get it boy." Dinner that night was in the bag. With a wry smile, Bob remembers trying to please the drivers and would curry favour by doing some really difficult and often dangerous jobs.

On one such occasion a driver was so pleased with Bob that he offered him a reward. Bob, thinking it would be enough to buy a pint, was really pleased. Imagine how he felt when the driver popped into the "Coffee Knob" and came out with a packet of Polo mints for him.

The Railway Club offered an opportunity for the odd illicit beer and a place where the drivers could relax and share their stories, though the younger lads tended to go farther afield for their fun.

After passing his exams, Bob became a "Passed Cleaner." Although this still meant mostly cleaning, with luck you could be called to do a firing turn. One memorable such shift was being caught up in the mayhem of the morning after the Great Train Robbery.

Passed Cleaner Bob is 2nd left, driver A Kerr and guard Pat Duffy.

On another occasion, Bob was out firing for Eddie Abbott. They made it as far as Rugby before snow set in to the point where they couldn't get back. This meant a 24 hour shift. That was OK in itself but to Bob's embarrassment his dad Gilbert Merivale came up to the station looking for him.

With a smile on his face, Bob recalls how that took a while to live down. Many will remember Bob's dad both for his years at the Bletchley Co-op as warehouse manager and for the many years he played the role of Father Christmas.

However, Bob hadn't been in the job for very long before it became obvious which way the wind was blowing. Insidiously, "diesel" began creeping in. Some of the lads stayed but industry was beginning to offer more opportunities.

Bob left to work at Bletchley Park, and for a while with the Electricity Board, before settling with Barclays Bank Stationery. In fact that is how many will remember him, his 30 years there and his role on the management team.

He will also be remembered by many local lads of the time for his love of motor bikes. Bob, a local biker, like many others enjoyed Mokaris café as a gathering place. His enthusiasm for motor bikes continued throughout his life.

Bob's railway days meant a lot to him and left a lasting impression. He recalls how it was a tight knit community; everyone knew everyone. It was a proud craft with proud men.

The passing of steam was the end of an era. It is an era that Bob remembers, purchasing the following photo from the offices of the Bletchley District Gazette.

The photo was clearly important to the young fireman, as in his own handwriting he has written on the back:

"Last steam engine off shed 5th July 1965
 Driver Harold Weaver, Fireman Eddie Hancock"

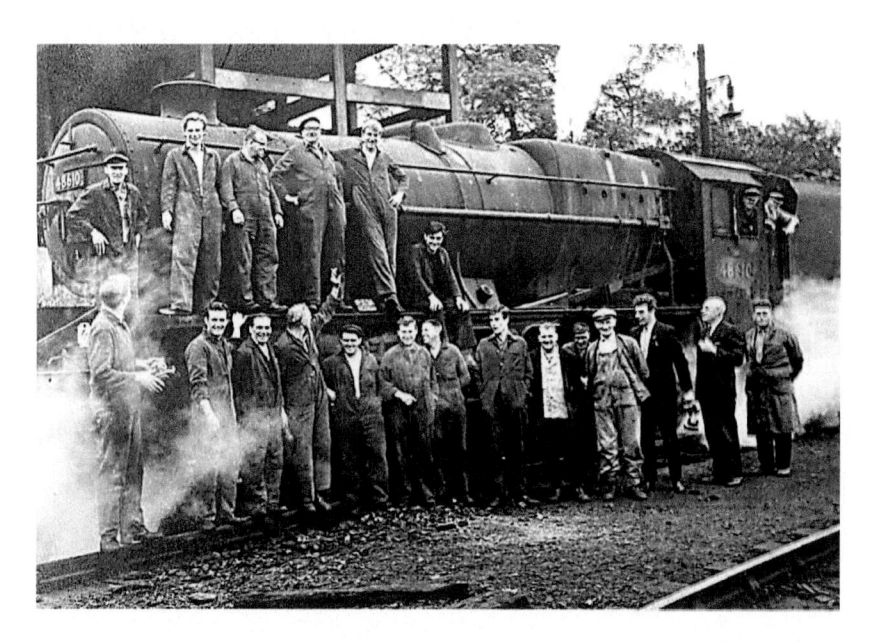

The passing of steam was indeed the end of an era.

Diane McLean

AFTERWORD

And so we regretfully close the lid on the memory box - for now at least.

This book has been a labour of love. Diane, Malcolm and I hope that you have enjoyed the contents.

I said in the introduction that wherever in the world we live, a part of our heart remains in Bletchley. I now live on South Island, New Zealand. I couldn't be further away geographically but you know where my heart is.

We are all too well aware that there are so many stories not included here, with more being added to the group daily. But we had to call a halt somewhere and after filling so many pages the end of an era seemed appropriate.

We are sorry if you couldn't find your favourites but you never know, if enough of you like this book there may yet be another down the line.

Here are the three of us. Sadly I live too far away to join Diane and Malcolm on the sofa. Jean Blane Flannery

Printed in Great Britain
by Amazon